Overtaken by Grace

How Intimacy with God Brings Hope, Healing, and Miracles

DEBBIE MILAM

Publisher's Cataloging-In-Publication Data
(Prepared by The Donohue Group, Inc.)

Names: Milam, Debbie.
Title: Overtaken by grace : how intimacy with God brings hope, healing and miracles / Debbie Milam.
Description: [Tampa, Florida] : Living Parables, [2017] | Includes a six-week Bible study. | Includes bibliographical references.
Identifiers: ISBN 978-1-941733-98-1 (print) | ISBN 978-1-941733-99-8 (ebook)
Subjects: LCSH: God (Christianity)--Attributes. | Hope--Religious aspects--Christianity. | Spiritual healing. | Miracles. | Christian life. | God (Christianity)--Biblical teaching. | BISAC: RELIGION / Christian Life / Inspirational. | RELIGION / Christian Life / Personal Growth. | RELIGION / Biblical Meditations / General.
Classification: LCC BT130 .M55 2017 (print) | LCC BT130 (ebook) | DDC 231.4--dc23

ISBN: 978-1-941733-98-1

Published by EA Books Publishing a division of
Living Parables of Central Florida, Inc. a 501c3

EABooksPublishing.com

Advance Praise for *Overtaken By Grace*

Overtaken by Grace is a beautifully written portrayal of the very nature of God. With honesty and transparency, Debbie Milam shares personal experiences that lead the reader to hunger and thirst for an intimate relationship with God. She puts a handle on God's promises and leads readers to apply them in their lives. *Overtaken by Grace* is both refreshing and challenging, a must-read for anyone struggling to find hope and light in the midst of despair and darkness. An added bonus is the Bible study for each chapter, making this book a perfect tool for small groups as well as personal study.

Mary Southerland
Cofounder of Girlfriends in God,
founder of Journey Ministry, international speaker,
and author of *Hope in the Midst of Depression*

An incredible reading experience. Debbie Milam takes you on personal journey embracing God's presence in the midst of challenges, uncertainty, and the moments that create complete havoc in your life. No matter what you are facing, *Overtaken by Grace* will encourage you and infuse soul-soothing insight. And through every carefully crafted thought, you will experience an endearing authenticity as Debbie's own spiritual journey with God is revealed.

Chris Trethewey
Senior pastor, Tri County Church, DuBois, Pennsylvania

Overtaken by Grace will take your faith to deeper levels and inspire you to see every part of life as a miracle. It is a refreshing read, using imagery that causes all of your senses to come alive in the presence of our heavenly Father. Gently inviting us to place every obstacle and pain into a view where God is at the center of it all, ready to carry us through the darkest moments of our life into His glorious light.

Suzanne Marcellus
Author of
Developing the Fruit of the Spirit: A Journey through the Heart of Christ

Debbie Milam has a heart that is Christ-centered and Kingdom-focused. Her words are insightful and uplifting to all who read them. I know that you will be inspired, encouraged, and challenged just as I have by this book. May God bless you in this reading.

Pastor Tommy Moseley
First Church of God, Wade, Mississippi

Overtaken by Grace is an intimate adventure with God that will refresh your soul as it reveals how God's promises bring comfort, peace, and healing throughout every season of your life. What an incredible book.

Lead Pastor Frank Toral
Promise Life Chapel

DEDICATION

To my extraordinary mother-in-law and spiritual momma, Joan,
thank you for showing me what intimacy with God looks like.

To Pastor Brian Vasil, thank you for all of your prayers, wisdom,
and encouragement to write this book.

CONTENTS

Introduction

What if that challenge—the one we cannot make go away, the one that overwhelms us—is a precious treasure, a gateway to God, to know His mercy, love, and grace? What if we begin to believe that His strength is made perfect in what we cannot do alone, and that we can, as Philippians 4:13 says, do all things through Christ who gives us strength? What if in the valley we truly believe in our victory? What if all *is* well—not because circumstances change but because of His love and goodness? Then will we fall into His grace, knowing that if we are experiencing a challenge, God invites us on the undertaking of a lifetime.

His invitation is for a deeper, more love-infused walk than we can imagine. In whatever trials we find ourselves, God is right beside us, His Holy Spirit alive within us. He knows how much we hurt and how confusing our circumstances often are. He sees our tears and knows our fears. Then His Word whispers, "Don't be afraid, for I am with you" (Isaiah 41:10, NLT).

Life is an adventure filled with various seasons and multiple peaks and valleys. Our family has rejoiced in the harvest of profound prosperity, healing, and blessing; weathered the uncertainty of trauma and physical and emotional illness; deeply

1

grieved the losses of more loved ones than I can count; and stood in awe at the continuous resurrection power of Christ in our lives. Life is a beautiful, messy, blessed, and sometimes broken glory road paved with love, tears, and faith. So, just as God invites us daily on a trust walk with Him, I invite you to pull up a chair, take off your shoes, and breathe deeply as I share my heart and how God epically shows up and shows off.

This is not a step-by-step way to move through adversity, although I wish there were one. This is not a self-help book, for in the deep waters, only God's grace redeems us. This is a book of hope—intimate essays that flowed from pen to paper after pouring out my pain to God and asking the Holy Spirit to pour into me.

Each page was crafted to encourage as our family walked through the joys and sorrows of life. During this journey I came to know a God that is alive, present, and loving. I came to know our Lord as healer, deliverer, wise counselor, and miracle maker. I was embraced by grace, overtaken by love, and bathed in comfort. I came to experience His power to overcome my problems, His grace to soothe my grief, and His wonder to trump my worry. The great paradox is that I came to know Him in all of these ways because of my need. We cannot experience a miracle until we need one. This is profoundly humbling. I sit in amazement that I, who was so wounded, could experience such wonder. Acts 10:34 proclaims, "God is no respecter of persons" (KJV). The same God who did this for me can do it for you. Let my testimony of the Lord's miraculous power expand your vision of what is possible. And as Matthew 19:26 declares, "With God all things are possible" (KJV).

While I do not know what you are walking through, God does. I simply share my personal journey and the resources that bless my life. I don't ask you to believe me or follow the same path I choose. I do invite you to deepen your relationship with the Lord and ask for His guidance on what is right in your circumstance and for your life.

My deepest prayer is that you know and experience the magnitude of His mercy, grandiosity of His grace, and luminosity of His love in your life experiences. Lord, bless every reader and reveal Yourself in and through these pages. In Jesus' name.

1

God's Presence in Our Lives

Made Whole

One day we awaken and acknowledge that hole in our soul — the one that came from loss or hurt; the one we try to fill in a plethora of ineffective ways with counterfeit comforts of food, drugs, worry, overdoing, the Internet, trying to control the uncontrollable, etc. One day we remember, that hole is in the shape of God. At that moment we realize the hole can become holy. Then as we ask God to fill us with His love, in time, He and only He makes us whole. First Thessalonians 5:23 says it all: "May God himself, the God who makes everything holy and whole, make you holy and whole, put you together — spirit, soul, and body" (MSG).

Thank you, Lord, that we are made whole in Your holy presence.

Where Is God?

People have often asked me where God is in the middle of their heartbreaks and personal challenges. I asked God this question frequently in the midst of my tears, anger, grieving, and healing from the tragedies our family experienced. The Lord reminded me that we live in a fallen world. At times our free will and the wounds of others cause the pain. Other times the consequences of our own choices contribute to our suffering. Finally, God allows challenges to occur to shape our character. The God I know does not bring tragedies; He brings us through them.

We are given a choice through our free will to find meaning and purpose, just as holocaust survivor and acclaimed author Viktor Frankl describes in *Man's Search for Meaning*. Here was a man in the depths of hell, confined to Nazi concentration camps, who made a conscious decision to give others hope. In that decision he found meaning and purpose, which Frank believed saved his life.[1]

The Bible is filled with stories of God's presence in the midst of human suffering, where His grace enabled broken people to rise above adversity and find meaning and purpose in their lives. Job, Joseph, and the writers of the book of Psalms all exemplify God's power and presence in human trials and how He brought good out of all of them. Challenges are part of life, and God uses every one of them to build our character, deepen our relationship with Him, and grow us into His masterpieces. Just as coal becomes a radiant diamond through pressure, we become all God has created us to be through our gifts as well as our trials and challenges.

I know from personal experience that God is ever-present—to comfort, love, bless, strengthen, and guide. He brought my family and me through many tragedies, trials, and losses and continues to bring beauty out of the ashes. My trials were more than many and less than others. Yet the strength, love, joy, peace, guidance, and comfort I find in the Bible and in His presence changed me much more than the challenges.

The 23rd psalm is a refuge during times of struggle:

> The Lord is my shepherd;
>
> I shall not want.
>
> He makes me to lie down in green pastures;
>
> He leads me beside the still waters.
>
> He restores my soul;
>
> He leads me in the paths of righteousness
>
> For His name's sake.
>
> Yea, though I walk through the valley of the shadow of death,
>
> I will fear no evil;
>
> For You are with me;
>
> Your rod and Your staff, they comfort me.
>
> You prepare a table before me in the presence of my enemies;
>
> You anoint my head with oil;
>
> My cup runs over.
>
> Surely goodness and mercy shall follow me
>
> All the days of my life;
>
> And I will dwell in the house of the Lord
>
> Forever. (NKJV)

Perhaps no other writing more clearly depicts the human experience and the power of God. There, in our challenge, lies a choice—a moment to turn to God and find healing, meaning, purpose, and comfort, or to turn away from Him. God is right beside us and knows what we are experiencing, and He is ready and able to grow us and carry us through. If we trust Him in the trial, all that He can birth within us is astonishing. Today, in whatever valley you find yourself, let this truth wash over you.

Walk through the valley with the goodness and mercy that await in the presence of the Lord.

Lord, help us to trust You right here, right now. We declare by faith that Your promises come to life.

God Is Able

Ephesians 3:20 reminds us that God is able to do "exceeding abundantly above all that we ask or think" (NKJV). So go to the well, drink from His living water, and let His grace and love pour over you. He's got this, but you must let go and follow His promptings rather than your emotions. Write out your worries, fears, guilt, shame, and circumstances and place them in your Bible or in a God box.

I've experienced moments when the only way I could unhook my mind from the anxiety was to write it down. In this surrender, a greater power arises. When I let go, God's power is manifest in and through me. If my hands, mind, and soul are filled with worry, doubt, condemnation, and unforgiveness, I block the flow of God's goodness and His perfect solution. For He sees the beginning from the end, and knows the perfect action to take. My intentional release and declaration of faith open a deeper level of trust, where I position myself to receive rather than block God's power.

I write this prayer, "Dear God, I surrender _____ to You and trust You are bringing good to and through it; show me what to do to move forward, be blessed, and be a blessing." First Peter 5:7 instructs us to cast our anxiety on Him because He cares. Trust Him that everything you are facing will work out—often better than you expected—when you let Him lead and obediently follow His promptings.

Thank you, God, that we can place everything in Your hands and help us to follow Your ways.

What God Does with Our Broken Pieces

One day I was in the middle of the morning rush driving my teenage daughter to school, preparing for a meeting, and feeling frazzled and weary. In moments like that, I know I must stop, breathe, and get in the presence of God. On the way home I stopped at a park where I had never been before. I was overtaken by the serenity and beauty—live oaks draped in Spanish moss, rolling meadows blanketed in emerald green, and banyan trees deeply rooted to the earth with arms outstretched to the heavens.

As I drove through the park, awed by God's magnificence, I saw an amazing oak tree. What astounded me was a heart-shaped scar left where a large branch had broken off. The scar did not take away from the beauty of the tree; it actually made the tree more beautiful.

Perhaps this is what God does with our scars. His love, grace, and mercy transform our broken pieces into something so much more beautiful.

Isaiah 61:3 soothes like a healing balm: "[God will] provide for those who grieve . . . to bestow on them a crown of beauty instead of ashes, the oil of joy instead of mourning, and a garment of praise instead of a spirit of despair. They will be called oaks of righteousness, a planting of the Lord for the display of his splendor" (NIV).

Thank you, Father, for how You transform all of our brokenness into something beautiful.

Experiencing the Love of God

God so loved us that He sent the world a part of Himself, His Son Jesus, as a baby. For when love came down in the form of an infant, the world got to experience God with us, Emmanuel. This presence of God's love is available to each of us. It is a love that is not dependent on how good we are, what religion we profess, or our status in the world. The love of Christ is available whether we feel worthy or unworthy. It is the same love regardless of how broken we feel, how many wrong choices we have made, whether we are addicted or hurt, or if we have hurt others.

God doesn't love us because of who we are but because of who He is. Not one of us could do anything to earn this love. We simply have to desire to be in relationship with the love that changes and transforms — in relationship with Christ. We are so loved that we are able to love more fully. A simple prayer inviting Jesus into your life and spending time in relationship with Him is the greatest gift you will ever receive.

So if you are ready to make Jesus the Lord of your life, pray this prayer: "Lord Jesus, I repent of my sins. Come into my heart. I make You my Lord and Savior."

God loves you so. Take a deep breath and allow that love to pour over you and bathe in His grace. For here in this space of love is where the deepest peace is found.

Thank you, God, that You love me no matter what.

How to Know God

I believe each of us has an innate desire to intimately know God. That intimacy begins when we enter into a relationship with Him through our salvation by faith in Jesus Christ. Yet so many believers feel separated from the One who created them. So how in our humanness do we move closer in our relationship with the majestic creator of the universe? The Bible gives a clear glimpse into one path to this intimacy:

Be still, and know that I am God.

Psalm 46:10, NIV

When I am still in His presence, immersed in the silence, a sacred communion arises — creator and creation, love and beloved. It is a profound worship experience to be still at the throne of grace. Present in the moment, I breathe deeply as if the Lord is breathing new life into my weary soul. I ask the Holy Spirit within to fill me with His unending love, to wash me in His goodness and bathe me in grace. In such moments I come to know our Lord as:

Calm in the storm

Grace in the moment

Wellspring of love

Still water of peace

Life-giving essence

Endless reservoir of guidance

Strength in our weakness

Joy in the trials

Blessings in the present

Comfort in the grief

Transforming and restoring mercy

Creator of all beauty . . .

For in the stillness, our intimacy with God dwells.

Psalm 46 reminds us that as we enter into stillness, we have an opportunity to know God—His peace, His comfort, His love. How different will your life and relationship with God be if each day you choose to spend moments of stillness in the presence of your creator? In order to have a relationship with anyone, you must spend time with that person. The same is true of our relationship with God.

One of my favorite practices is the Be Still scripture meditation I learned from a sister in the faith. A version of this also appears in Ken Blanchard's book *Lead Like Jesus*.[2]

The Hebrew word for meditation is hagah, which means to speak. After each breath repeat the phrase either aloud or in the quiet of your mind:

Breathe in: "Be still and know that I am God.

Breathe out: "Be still and know."

Breathe in: "Be still."

Breathe out: "Be."

As we breathe, we relax our bodies to connect deeper to the presence of God. Job 33:4 beautifully illustrates this: "The Spirit of God has made me; and the breath of the Almighty gives me life" (NIV).

Enjoy the stillness. Enjoy the presence of God. After being refreshed in quiet communion, share your heart with God and ask the Holy Spirit to guide you throughout your day. God so loves communion.

Thank you, Lord, that Your Word invites us to be still in Your presence – to know You and Your lavish love.

Not Religion

What religion do I have to practice to know God? Can going to church make my problems go away? I have asked the Lord and myself these questions many times. Yet I am reminded that the blessing of knowing God is not about religion but about relationship. Religion cannot turn fear into faith; only Christ can. Religion cannot comfort the grieving; only the Holy Spirit can. Religion cannot bring good out of suffering; only an indwelling, radiant, living God can do that. Religion cannot offer forgiveness; only the grace of Jesus can forgive us and He blesses us to forgive others.

As a seeker my whole life, I looked for God in every religion. Although each faith had something beautiful to offer, nothing satisfied the deep longing until I met my Lord and Savior, Jesus Christ. You do not need to be part of a religion to be in a living relationship with Jesus. You simply have to invite Him into your life.

May you experience the fullness of God's love and grace as you walk through the joys and trials in your life.

2

God's Love in Our Relationships

Real Love

How do we love when others or we are hurt, acting out, in pain, or just being human? The Bible reveals a divine formula in 1 John 4:19: "We love because He first loved us" (NIV). We cannot give what we do not have; an empty well can give no water. As we awaken, before we encounter others, we are given a choice to be like Mary and sit at the feet of Jesus—worshiping Him, praying, and allowing His divine love to overtake us—or to be like Martha—busy, solving problems, fixing things in our own strength (see Luke 10:38–42). Our choice is either to plunge into His endless well of mercy and power or to plug into the news, the Internet, or the problem du jour. Some days it is easy to make the wise choice for God. Regrettably, at other times, the pull of distraction feels larger than the call of my Savior.

Mark 12:30 gives clear direction in making our choice. We are first to love the Lord our God with all of our hearts and minds, our souls and our strength; then we can love our neighbors as ourselves. Being in the presence of God, letting Him love us through His Word and His Holy Spirit, is how we can then love those around us. God's perfect instruction for real love is revealed in 1 Corinthians 13:4–8: "Love is patient and kind. Love is not jealous or boastful or proud or rude. It does not demand its own way. It is not irritable, and it keeps no record of being wronged. It does not rejoice about injustice but rejoices whenever the truth wins out. Love never gives up, never loses faith, is always hopeful, and endures through every circumstance" (NLT).

We are called to walk in the way of love (see Ephesians 5:2, NIV). First John 4:18 takes it even deeper: "There is no fear in love; but perfect love casts out fear" (NKJV). A tall order, and one I continually need the Lord's help with to grow. Yet we are able to love in this way when we surrender our worry, fear, and resentment and ask God to show us how to love as He loves. A priceless gift.

Dear God, bless us and show us how to experience the gift of Your astonishing agape love so that all we give to others is Your love in and through us.

Parenting Teens

Perhaps the most challenging and rewarding moments in life involve parenting a teen. As I have witnessed and enmeshed myself in my children's growth, I am continually reminded that I am not in charge. My beloved creator brought these beautiful children to and through me so I could teach them. But more important, so that they could teach me how to trust God.

Ultimately my children are not mine. I do not have ownership but I can guide them. I do not know what God plans for their lives, but I can be their mentor. I cannot protect them from life's valleys, but I lovingly walk beside them. I cannot stop their choices that I judge harmful, but I can discipline, set boundaries, and at times get them professional help. My children are God's children entrusted to me to love, nurture, discipline, train, and assist Him in raising.

When they struggle, although my desire is for their circumstances to be easier, I have an opportunity to grow in faith, trust, and patience. I trust that God is walking right beside them and will guide me to take the right actions as a parent. I need patience to allow their growth to unfold.

This is a walk I surely cannot do alone. As a recovering worrier, I need an army of warriors—prayer partners who remind me of the goodness of God and pray in agreement that God is in control and I can trust Him. These blessed friends come alongside to help me remember that God's plans for my children are to prosper them and not harm them, to give them hope and a future (see Jeremiah 29:11).

With bended knee I cry out to my Lord, who loves my children even more than I. He pours His mercy upon me and renews my mind, soothes my soul, shifts my perspective, and gives me supernatural guidance.

As a parent, my greatest power comes from the greatest power of all—my God. As I join my heart to the heart of my heavenly

Father through His scriptures, and seeking His guidance through being in His presence, I turn in the direction of God's promises for my children. I pray and ask God to help my teens experience His promises—those that are specific to their unique needs. This is not my opportunity to fix them but to stand in agreement with God's plan for their lives. Scriptures that speak of listening to God's guidance, being who God calls them to be, developing character, being blessed, and being surrounded by a hedge of protection are among many desires I pray for my children. Pouring my hopes, dreams, and fears before the Lord not only calms my heart but also plants supernatural seeds where I can focus on their potential rather than just on their problems—especially during times of growth.

One day in particular stands out. I was sitting in Bible study overrun with angst about my teenager. Our Bible study teacher had asked me to read Psalm 139 as part of our study on the power of God. As I read the words I began to weep, for His Word was speaking directly to my fearful mind. I have continued to read this psalm many times. When concern over my children, myself, or other people I love arises, I place their names where the psalmist refers to himself. Here it is:

GOD, investigate my life;

> get all the facts firsthand.

I'm an open book to you;

> even from a distance, you know what I'm thinking.

You know when I leave and when I get back;

> I'm never out of your sight,

You know everything I'm going to say

> before I start the first sentence.

I look behind me and you're there,

> then up ahead and you're there, too—

> your reassuring presence, coming and going.

This is too much, too wonderful—

    I can't take it all in!

Is there anyplace I can go to avoid your Spirit?

    to be out of your sight?

If I climb to the sky, you're there!

    If I go underground, you're there!

If I flew on morning's wings

    to the far western horizon,

You'd find me in a minute—

    you're already there waiting!

Then I said to myself, "Oh, he even sees me in the dark!

    At night I'm immersed in the light!"

It's a fact: darkness isn't dark to you;

    night and day, darkness and light, they're all the same to you.

Oh yes, you shaped me first inside, then out;

    you formed me in my mother's womb.

I thank you, High God—you're breathtaking!

    Body and soul, I am marvelously made!

    I worship in adoration—what a creation!

You know me inside and out,

    you know every bone in my body;

You know exactly how I was made, bit by bit,

    how I was sculpted from nothing into something.

Like an open book, you watched me grow from conception to birth;

    all the stages of my life were spread out before you,

The days of my life all prepared

before I'd even lived one day.

Your thoughts—how rare, how beautiful!

God, I'll never comprehend them!

I couldn't even begin to count them—

any more than I could count the sand of the sea.

Oh, let me rise in the morning and live always with you!

And please, God, do away with wickedness for good!

Psalm 139:1–19, MSG

When I keep my perspective on God's ways, I see that my children are not struggling but growing. I accept that I cannot predict the outcome of their lives, but my beloved creator reminds me that all is well and He is with them.

The teenage years are similar to the great metamorphosis of nature's most precious gift, a butterfly. The faith, trust, and patience the Lord gives me keeps me from wanting to cut my children out of their cocoon and rescue them from pain. If this were done to a caterpillar, it would never have the opportunity to transform, as only God can accomplish, into a majestic butterfly. Likewise, the profound gift in witnessing my children's growth is that I too welcome God's transformation of my heart and mind.

Thank you, Lord, that Your hand is upon my children and You are blessing them to be a blessing.

When Your Plans Take a Detour

Emily Kingsley, writer for *Sesame Street*, penned one of my favorite poems. She describes a woman who's planning a trip to Italy. She did everything she could to prepare for this journey. She learned Italian, bought new clothes, and researched activities in which to participate when she arrived. She was completely ready for Italy.

Her excitement grew as she boarded the plane. At the end of the long flight, the stewardess announced, "Welcome to Holland." The woman protested, "I'm not going to Holland. I'm going to Italy." The flight attendant gently repeated, "Welcome to Holland."

She left the plane frustrated and angry. As she walked through the airport, still irate, she looked outside and noticed windmills, tulips, and beautiful rolling hills of emerald green. Although she mourned the loss of her dream, she saw that Holland was beautiful. Clearly, she could enjoy herself there.

Kingsley went on to share that this was what it was like raising a child with special needs. Her son was born with Down Syndrome. Through this journey she has inspired millions of moms of special needs kids, including me, with her poem "Welcome to Holland." She also incorporated issues of disability acceptance into multiple segments on *Sesame Street*.[3] Her "purpose" was revealed through this part of her journey.

How many times in our own lives do we plan and tell God where we want to go, how we want our lives to be, or how we want the lives of our loved ones to be? Jeremiah 29:11 reminds us, "'For I know the plans I have for you,' declares the LORD, 'plans to prosper you and not harm you, plans to give you hope and a future'" (NIV).

This passage teaches us that there are times when we cannot control the circumstances of our lives; we can only control how we move through them. God has a plan right in the middle of our life experience. His purpose is greater than anything our human eyes can see. What we can control is our attitude.

A profound choice point arises when we change our attitude from "Why me, Lord?" to "What now, Lord? What is Your purpose in this, and how can I bless others through it?" Our perception shifts from one of fear to one of faith. That is when God can do the mightiest work within us and through us. I have seen, time and time again, unexpected blessings pour out of circumstances that from my own human perception look and feel like suffering. But through the power and the glory of God, we can trust that all things work together for good (see Romans 8:28).

Wherever your journey takes you, grab the hand of a prayer partner and the Holy Spirit as your travel companions. Pack your bag full of encouraging and faith-filled scriptures. See the beauty, the blessing, and God in all things. As you walk by faith and not by sight (see 2 Corinthians 5:7), your life becomes an adventure of possibility and purpose wherever your path leads.

Lord, guide our ways. Let us see our lives through Your eyes of grace, and help us to remember that Your detours may just be our destiny.

The Grace of Forgiveness

Grace=Forgiveness

As Christians we are given the greatest, most precious gift—grace, the forgiveness of our sins through the sacrifice and love of our savior, Jesus Christ. When Jesus died on the cross, the divine exchange occurred where He bore all of our sin, shame, pain, and wounds. In that moment on Calvary two thousand years ago, I was forgiven, each of you was forgiven, and (this is hard to hear), every person who betrayed us, angered us, hurt us, or abused us was also forgiven. "He suffered and endured great pain for us, but we thought his suffering was punishment from God. He was wounded and crushed because of our sins; by taking our punishment he made us completely well" (Isaiah 53:4-5, CEV).

Jesus already paid the price for us to be free. Our part is to focus on the renewal of our mind and the walking out of our faith to step into the forgiveness God already provided so we can live free. Still, in our humanness, many of us do not live free. We carry resentments, pain, hurt, and unforgiveness.

If God has forgiven us and every other person, why do we hold on to the pain?

Some of our pain is front and center; other parts are buried deep. As you embark on this forgiveness adventure, know the Lord is with you. You may feel difficult emotions. You may, if your wounds are deep from trauma like mine were, need the support of a counselor. The journey of forgiveness is between you and God. I am only here to share what the Lord taught me in my own walk and how He blessed me in the process.

As we enter into this living relationship with the God of all grace, we are called to forgive others as we have been forgiven (see Ephesians 4:32). Yet the process of forgiveness is painful because it involves our human frailty and wounds.

The word *forgive* in the Greek translation means "to release a burden"; in Hebrew it means "to be carried by the wind." To forgive is to let go.

Forgiveness is like an onion—as you peel away the layers it is uncomfortable. There are tears, but when put together with additional ingredients, including faith and compassion, it becomes a delicious recipe for our lives. Wouldn't it be wonderful if we could forgive once and be done with it? God's Word reminds us that we have to forgive over and over again:

Peter: Lord, when someone has sinned against me, how many times ought I forgive him? *Once? Twice?* As many as seven times?

Jesus: You must forgive not seven times, but seventy times seven.

Matthew 18:21–22, VOICE

Each time we forgive, a deeper level of truth, peace, and compassion is revealed. Each layer emerges when we are ready— when we feel safe enough to explore. Forgiveness is not something we do for another. Through forgiveness we experience the freedom Christ died for so that we can live free and experience His love. Forgiveness is only between you and God.

There are two aspects of forgiveness: forgiving ourselves and forgiving others. You may wonder why you should forgive yourself. Because you are so precious to God that He wants you to be free from the burden of any resentment. His Word gives us many truths about our significance to God, our creator:

"I have loved you with an everlasting love;
I have drawn you with unfailing kindness."

Jeremiah 31:3, NIV

For you are a people holy to the LORD your God. The LORD your God has chosen you out of all the peoples on the face of the earth to be his people, his treasured possession.

Deuteronomy 7:6, NIV

For we are God's masterpiece. He has created us anew in Christ Jesus, so we can do the good things he planned for us long ago.

Ephesians 2:10, NLT

You made all the delicate, inner parts of my body
  and knit me together in my mother's womb.
Thank you for making me so wonderfully complex!
  Your workmanship is marvelous—how well I know it.

Psalm 139:13–14, NLT

God created us as amazing masterpieces, and although we fall short, sin, and need a savior, we are His precious children, and He offers us the magnificent gift of forgiveness, just as Jesus did in Luke 7:47–48:

Jesus, speaking to the accusers of the sinful woman who wet Jesus' feet with her tears, dried them with her hair, and anointed them with perfume: "Therefore I tell you, her sins, which are many, are forgiven—for she loved much. But he who is forgiven little, loves little." And he said to her, "Your sins are forgiven." (ESV)

How can we love anyone else if we don't love the precious creations He called us to be?

Now let's take it a step further. Why do we need to forgive others? Take a moment to meditate on the same truths in these scriptures again. As you do, think of those who have hurt or angered you, and how God feels about them:

"I have loved you with an everlasting love;
I have drawn you with unfailing kindness."

Jeremiah 31:3, NIV

For you are a people holy to the LORD your God. The LORD your God has chosen you out of all the peoples on the face of the earth to be his people, his treasured possession.

Deuteronomy 7:6, NIV

For we are God's masterpiece. He has created us anew in Christ Jesus, so we can do the good things he planned for us long ago.

Ephesians 2:10, NLT

You made all the delicate, inner parts of my body
and knit me together in my mother's womb.
Thank you for making me so wonderfully complex!
Your workmanship is marvelous—how well I know it.

Psalm 139:13–14, NLT

Astonishing when we remember who we are and who others truly are in Christ. Yet there are deeper reasons to forgive. Ephesians 4:26–27 gives us another insight: "Don't let the sun go down while you are still angry, for anger gives a foothold to the devil" (NLT). Do you really want to give the enemy any foothold in your life?

Matthew 6:9–13 clearly shows in the Sermon on the Mount that forgiveness precedes deliverance from temptation and the evil one:

Our Father in heaven,
Reveal who you are.
Set the world right;
Do what's best—
     as above, so below.
Keep us alive with three square meals.
Keep us forgiven with you and forgiving others.
Keep us safe from ourselves and the Devil.
You're in charge!
You can do anything you want!
You're ablaze in beauty! (MSG)

Finally, 2 Corinthians 2:5–8 is a life-changing call to action. "Now if anyone has caused pain, he has caused it not to me, but in some measure — not to put it too severely — to all of you. For such a one, this punishment by the majority is enough, so you should rather turn to forgive and comfort him, or he may be overwhelmed by excessive sorrow. So I beg you to reaffirm your love for him" (ESV).

So how in our humanness and our hurt do we experience the sacred, holy embrace of grace? How do we forgive? After a series of events that brought me to my knees, I cried out to the Lord, asking Him how to forgive. In His sweet mercy He overtook my pain with this process of forgiveness. Here is the process He gifted me with to forgive, using the acrostic for GRACE:

G — Go to God

For many of us, the process of forgiveness seems daunting, yet our heavenly Father is there to guide and love us by giving us mercy and grace to forgive. The Voice gives us a clear directive: "So let us step boldly to the throne of grace, where we can find mercy and grace to help when we need it most" (Hebrews 4:16).

Forgiveness is one of those areas in my life that I cannot do alone. What stops you from asking for God's help? What lies does the enemy, or your inner mind, tell you about yourself and why you can't ask for God's help? He has a message for you in these times. "Are you tired? Worn out? Burned out on religion? Come to me. Get away with me and you'll recover your life. I'll show you how to take a real rest. Walk with me and work with me — watch how I do it. Learn the unforced rhythms of grace. I won't lay anything heavy or ill-fitting on you. Keep company with me and you'll learn to live freely and lightly" (Matthew 11:28–30, MSG). The times when we are most burdened yet we bring those burdens to God are the times we most feel His presence and His power.

R — Release

Anger, fear, sadness, and resentment are all human emotions. Jesus experienced all of these in His humanity. Even the Bible validates our angry feelings, as Ephesians 4:26 reminds us, "Be angry and do not sin" (ESV).

The freedom from these emotions comes when we lay them all on the cross. Emotions placed at the feet of Jesus are transformed, transfigured, and transmuted. The release of these feelings can occur by pouring your heart out to God either aloud in prayer or on paper. Forgiveness without releasing the feelings is only partial. God created us with feelings. The trouble comes not from feeling emotions but letting them guide our actions and control us.

Psalm 55:22 reminds us of the sustaining power our Lord provides when we bring our emotions to Him. "Cast your cares on the Lord, and he will sustain you; he will never let the righteous be shaken" (NIV). Even when we feel shaky in our feelings, when we feel them in the presence of God we are not shaken.

Sometimes we are angry with the other person — other times with ourselves. We can hold resentment against a circumstance, an institution, an ideal, a place, or a person. At some moments we are angry with God. More often than not, several factors play into our anger and hurt. Yet when you are in an alive, intimate relationship with the Lord, He loves and accepts all of you. When we honestly share and submit to Him, we are open to receive His grace. For as Romans 8:1 so eloquently expresses, "Therefore, there is now no condemnation for those who are in Christ Jesus" (NIV).

A — Awareness/Acceptance

Once our feelings are shared with the Lord of all grace, He opens us up with compassion. We accept and become aware that those we have anger toward did their best at the level of awareness they could achieve. Luke 23:34 illustrates this perfectly. As Jesus hangs on the cross facing the greatest pain of His life, He prays, "Father, forgive them, for they don't know what they are doing" (NLT).

Once we accept the limitations of others, we move to the acceptance of God's will. If He allowed a circumstance in our lives, He can use it to grow us through it. As we follow His will, we are called to dress in the garment God picked for us. Colossians 3:13–14 describes this new wardrobe: "So, chosen by God for this new life of love, dress in the wardrobe God picked out for you: compassion, kindness, humility, quiet strength, discipline. Be even-tempered, content with second place, quick to forgive an offense. Forgive as quickly and completely as the Master forgave you. And regardless of what else you put on, wear love. It's your basic, all-purpose garment. Never be without it" (MSG).

Be mindful that if you are in an abusive situation, seek professional advice and help. Forgiveness and acceptance do not mean putting yourself in harm's way. Ever!

C – Change in Perception

After the Lord blesses us with acceptance and awareness, He will renew our minds through a change in our perception. When we ask God, "Why did this happen *for* me? What is Your purpose for this and how can I glorify You in this?" rather than "Why did this happen *to* me?" we are moved into a position of power — from victim to victor. The Holy Spirit empowers us to see our circumstances through eyes of grace.

Philippians 1:19 echoes this promise. "For I know that through your prayers and God's provision of the Spirit of Jesus Christ what has happened to me will turn out for my deliverance" (NIV). This verse reminds us that our pain serves a purpose, and that it is not punishment but preparation, and perhaps even a part of our calling.

E—Even Though It Hurts, Give Thanks

Knowing the power of the King of Mercy to orchestrate everything to work together for our good, we give thanks for true forgiveness when we say, "Lord, thank you for giving me the experience." Even in the most painful of circumstances, God births within us the gifts of courage, strength, endurance, and patience. For all these things we express gratefulness. First Thessalonians 5:18 reminds us, "Give thanks to God no matter what circumstances you find yourself in. (This is God's will for all of you in Jesus the Anointed)" (VOICE).

After exercising this forgiveness process around some areas of shame and pain in my own life, I rededicated myself to Christ in the same pool in which I was baptized. As I emerged from the water, the sky was alight with vapor trails that formed an enormous cross above my house. The same breed of butterflies we released in our yard to celebrate my baptism danced by my nose. Later that day I received a delivery of flowers from a friend just because she loved me, and I also opened several emails of affirmation. A coincidence—no. A God incident— yes.

Once we forgive and release our shame, blame, guilt, hurt, sadness, and anger, we make space for greater gifts. And the richest gift of all is the freedom and love we find in the Lord Christ Jesus.

Thank you, Lord, that I am forgiven and loved, and so is everyone else.

3

God's Peace in Our Emotions

The Gift in the Grief

Although each of us has different journeys, all of us will experience loss. It is part of the human experience. That loss may be the loss of a loved one, the loss of a dream, the loss of health, or challenges of many kinds.

When grief touches you, know that God is right beside you to guide you, carry you, comfort you, and love you. He understands. Our Lord Jesus was a man of sorrow—acquainted with grief (see Isaiah 53:3).

Some time ago, after I received the news of the passing of a loved one, several scriptures flashed across the TV. Yes, I was watching Christian television. I knew at that moment God was reminding me to stand on the promises of His Word. As I felt the sadness, in His presence I was washed in His love. Here are the words that blessed me so:

> You're blessed when you feel you've lost what is most dear to you. Only then can you be embraced by the One most dear to you.
>
> Matthew 5:4, MSG

[For those who grieve, God will] bestow on them a crown of beauty instead of ashes, the oil of joy instead of mourning, and a garment of praise instead of a spirit of despair.

Isaiah 61:3, NIV

So those who went off with heavy hearts will come home laughing, with armloads of blessing.

Psalm 126:66, MSG

You did it: You turned my deepest pains into joyful dancing; You stripped off my dark clothing and covered me with joyful light.

Psalm 30:11, VOICE

Bringing the grief, tears, and brokenness to the Lord not only heals us but also opens us up to a love beyond measure — the love of God. His Word is alive with hope and the promise of healing — a brighter tomorrow in the middle of the grieving process.

If only grief were a one-and-done event. Yet like all spiritual growth, it is a process. It takes great courage to walk into the deep waters of grief — to enter the abyss. At times the grieving feels like ocean waves coming onshore. Some waves are calm; others are as strong as a tsunami and feel as if they will take you under. The waves can be fear, anger, sadness, despair, weariness, confusion, and/or apathy. Nevertheless, just like ocean waves, once they subside you emerge. The good news is that buried treasures are revealed in the deep. An inner resiliency surfaces — God's strength in our weakness comes to life. We grow in grace, courage, compassion, and love. As we face loss, life becomes an even more precious gift.

Just as you should never swim alone in the ocean, walking through grief alone is unhealthy. Find some loving friends, a support group like GriefShare, a good therapist, or a pastoral counselor.

Get out your tissues. Go to God. Let it out—all the tears and sadness. As your tears fall like rain, remember John 11:35, "Jesus wept." Your Lord knows how deep the pain is. In His grief He went off to be alone with the Father for comfort. We can do the same by reading His Word, especially the psalms, and filling ourselves with His promises. They bring life. Give yourself permission to feel in the presence of God. It is truly an act of love that gives birth to a greater intimacy and healing.

Remember, you are never alone; God is right beside you. Ask Him to show you that He is there in a way you can understand and trust.

Thank you, God, for tears that cleanse our souls. Your Word is like a holy tissue. Your love comforts us as we mourn.

It Is Well with My Soul

We may never fully understand why we experience the circumstances we do, but God does understand. In His infinite grace and glory, He allows the circumstances of our lives to unfold in order to help us grow in character, deepen our walk with Him, and inspire others on their life journeys.

Horatio Spafford was one of the people God used. In a two-year period he went from being a successful attorney with a beautiful family to losing all his wealth due to the Chicago fires. He witnessed five of his children die—one from rheumatic fever and four in an accident. The depth of his loss was beyond tragic, but Horatio knew a deeper walk with God.

In the depths of his pain, he cried out to the Lord and experienced God's supernatural peace—a peace that passed all understanding (see Philippians 4:7). Being still in the presence of God, he sat down and penned the words to "It Is Well with My Soul," perhaps one of the greatest hymns of all times. Did he still grieve? Of course. Yet through his life experience God brought him peace and comfort, not just to Spafford but to millions for the past 140 years.

We may never have the influence of Horatio Spafford, yet we all have experiences that can touch another. Are you ready to let God turn your mess into a message of hope? Your test into your testimony? Your trial into God's triumph? Second Corinthians 1:3-4 unpacks this truth: "Praise be to God and Father of our Lord Jesus Christ, the Father of compassion and the God of all comfort, who comfort us in all our troubles, so that we can comfort those in any trouble with the comfort we ourselves receive from God" (NIV). So go to Him in prayer and be still in His presence. In the shelter of God's love you can know that whatever you experience, with His compassion and comfort, you can trust that in time it will be well with your soul.

Dear God, help us to experience Your truth that "it is well," for You are our well. As we are so richly blessed, help us to be a blessing to others.

Stress

Stress occurs when the demands of an experience outweigh our perceived resources. God never gives us more than we can handle without Him—just more than we can control.

Matthew 19:26 says, "With man this is impossible, but with God all things are possible." Today, remember that God gives us an infinite well of strength, guidance, and most of all, love. We never, ever have to do anything alone. Go to Him often and say, "Lord, I need Your help. Show me how to experience Your victory in a way that will glorify You and bless others." He is waiting with open arms, delights in your asking, and will infuse you with His strength to move through the joys and challenges of this abundant life.

Oh dear God, thank you that at any moment we can make the choice to place all of the stress into Your loving hands. Help us to remember that we may need to do this over and over again. And once we let go, we can then clearly hear Your guidance and receive Your love.

Worry

> Don't worry about anything; instead, pray about
> everything; tell God your needs, and don't forget to thank
> him for his answers. If you do this, you will experience
> God's peace, which is far more wonderful than the human
> mind can understand. His peace will keep your thoughts
> and your hearts quiet and at rest as you trust in Christ
> Jesus.
>
> Philippians 4:6–7, TLB

The full power of this passage is letting go and letting God. As
you tell God what you need, you are letting go. In the letting go,
the clarity and discernment to take right action comes from the
Holy Spirit who is alive within you. The key is to become quiet
enough to listen. When my mind is at peace and fully connected
to the One who sees the bigger picture, to an all-knowing and all-
loving God, answers arise that from my own human perspective, I
would not see.

Pause, breathe, pray, thank —
experience peace and trust.

In the past, I have experienced the overwhelming anxiety that
came from living, during a period of time, with the effects of
posttraumatic stress disorder. As a recovering worrier, the above
words bring comfort to my soul. I used to think worry was an
emotion. Today it is crystal clear that worry is a behavior. As with
all behaviors, God gives us a choice. We can continue the behavior
that is unhealthy, or we can give it to Him to transform into His
peace and serenity.

God so lovingly knows that the human mind slips into worry.
Yet His Word soothes us, reminding us that our loving Father
says, *"Do not worry, I am here."*

Pause, breathe, pray, thank —
experience peace and trust.

38

Worry is a form of control that gives us something to do. Because God has given us free will, He allows us to continue forcing solutions, trying to figure things out, and running the endless tape of various scenarios again and again in our minds. Yet when we place our worried thoughts in the hands of Jesus, we find profound peace. From this place of peace we are able to take right action, if any is needed. Through His peace, when I turned my anxiety over to God, He guided me to the right therapists, who with God's grace gave me freedom from the pain of the past.

If you are ready to experience God's serenity, which is far more wonderful than the human mind can comprehend, take time to pause, breathe, pray, thank — experience peace and trust. Let go and let God. He is here and "able to do exceeding abundantly above all that we ask or think" (Ephesians 3:20, KJV).

Thank you, Lord, that You are here, that I can breathe. Help me to let go and trust You.

This Too Shall Pass

Breathe, dear one. Rest in His love and His Word, and know this too shall pass. Just as day turns to night and night back to day, circumstances also change. In the middle of uncertainty we crave certainty, yet the only thing to be completely certain of is God's infinite love and His promises over your life.

He knows you are hurting and He is your comfort. First Peter 5:10 soothes the weary soul: "And the God of all grace, who called you to his eternal glory in Christ, after you have suffered a little while, will himself restore you and make you strong, firm and steadfast" (NIV).

How wonderful the hope of His Word. We serve a God who specializes in renewal, redemption, and grace. This hope, the hope of Christ, is yours, a bright morning star to illuminate your path and make a way through the dark night of your soul.

Thank you, God, that You are a beacon of light and I can trust in You and Your power.

Hope in All Things

> So those who went off with heavy hearts will come home
> laughing, with armloads of blessing.
>
> Psalm 126:5, MSG

This scripture brought so much hope to one of the darkest times in our family. *Can it be true?* I cried intensely as I read and absorbed this promise. Then, through tear-filled cries, I uttered, "God, if this is true, show me how to experience this." In moments of heaviness, of weariness, I asked again and again. Slowly the veil of heaviness, the cloak of despair, began to lift. Praise God, His promise was true.

Out of the depths of pain, blessings are birthed. Weeping turns to laughter — all by His grace. Is it easy? No. Is it possible? Yes. As I look back at our many grief journeys, God has been faithful, and hope abounds in His holy Word. I love this acrostic for HOPE:

H — hold

O — on

P — pain

E — ends

Whatever you are experiencing, know there is a fully present, loving God right beside you and inside you. Your loving Father knows the beginning from the end, and He has a plan and a purpose right in the middle of what you are experiencing. Through His grace there is victory and blessing on the other side. Beloved, if you are still here, praise Him, for He has either carried you through or is about to. Hold on, dear one, pain ends.

Will it take work on your part? You bet it will. Is it worth it? Absolutely. You are worth it.

Thank you, God, that Your Word washes grief, Your promises provide hope, and You are right here with me.

Get Comfortable with Being Uncomfortable

As I arise and greet the dawn, I thank God for breathing life back into my soul. Although I know the fullness of God's grace and love, I am also well acquainted with the fullness of my anxious mind. I call out to my beloved Lord, "Please show me how to move back into Your peace." I am guided to bring pen to paper, surrender the ramblings of my mind to my holy Father, and seek His guidance.

As I empty out my anxiety onto the page, I hear storm clouds release what is pent up within them. Then the rain begins to fall. The Holy Spirit speaks to my heart, *"Walk out into the rain, sweet child."* I reply in my heart, *I do not like to be wet and uncomfortable.* My beloved Lord gently encourages me, *"Little one, grab a raincoat and walk with me."* Obedient, I venture out. Indeed, the rain is pelting my face and pants, but my jacket is keeping my upper torso dry and cozy.

What if in times of anxiety I remember God is my raincoat of strength, security, and warmth? What if I remember that any time I feel vulnerable by the changing elements of life, I can don this God-coat, wrap myself in divine grace, and find comfort in His presence?

As I continue my walk, my anxiety begins to abate. My breathing becomes deeper and more rhythmic, and my soul quiets down. The rain now becomes a paintbrush on the canvas of the trees, the lake, and the flowers. Light dances through the drops of moisture, and the healing rain quenches the parched blanket of emerald that lays gently upon the earth. As heaven's showers fall, the earth welcomes the change, for the rain is as essential as the sun.

In our day-to-day walk with the Lord, the same is true. The blessings of joy, love, well-being, and prosperity—although far more fun than the challenges—are of no greater value. The victory and the abundant life are not found in our circumstances; they are found in the relationship we share with Christ, ourselves, and each other. Each experience God brings to us and through us is an opportunity for good and growth—an opportunity to draw nearer to His love. Paul, in his letter to the Corinthians, expresses this eloquently:

> So we're not giving up. How could we! Even though on the outside it often looks like things are falling apart on us, on the inside, where God is making new life, not a day goes by without his unfolding grace. These hard times are small potatoes compared to the coming good times, the lavish celebration prepared for us. There's far more here than meets the eye. The things we see now are here today, gone tomorrow. But the things we can't see now will last forever.
>
> 2 Corinthians 4:17–18, MSG

As this awareness arises, the blessing of the storm reveals itself. The sky is illuminated with a symphony of colors. A full arc rainbow emerges from the storm clouds. Surely when we choose to walk hand-in-hand with our beloved Lord, oh, the magnificent beauty we experience in any weather.

Thank you, God, that everything within me and before me is for good and for growth if I choose it to be.

When You Are Weary

One of my favorite things to do as a child was to turn down the lights, grab a fluffy blanket, and rest. Today I have that same opportunity with my heavenly Father.

In a world that is overcommitted to doing, staying connected, and nonstop chatter, I make a conscious commitment to rest in the arms of my beloved creator.

As the fullness of life expands, so does my need for the fullness of His rest. I am reminded that I am a human being, not a human doing. When the busyness of life becomes overwhelming, there is an infinite well of renewing living water. Here I can rest by the still waters of His majesty. Here I become embraced by His love.

Moment by moment I remember that I can be refreshed before I am overwhelmed, simply because I love the Lord and myself enough to relax in the stillness — in His presence.

> Come to me, all you who are weary and burdened, and I will give you rest. For my yoke is easy and my burden is light.
>
> Matthew 11:28, 30, NIV

I humbly and joyfully accept this invitation. Resting in the arms of my heavenly Father, I am enveloped in love, wrapped in grace, and filled with peace in a way I cannot achieve alone. I am renewed, restored, and rejuvenated.

An acrostic for REST reawakens me to the gifts that come from consciously choosing to enjoy moments of stillness:

R — retreat into silence

E — enter into prayer

S — surrender to His love

T — trust in His grace

Whatever you are experiencing in your life, resting in the peace of God's presence will give you clarity to move through life with greater grace, open you to the gifts alive in the present moment, and enrich your life in more ways than you can imagine.

Thank you, Lord, that in the fullness of life is the fullness of Your peace as we rest in You.

Rise Up

> Sovereign LORD, you are God! Your covenant is trustworthy, and you have promised these good things to your servant.
>
> 2 Samuel 7:28, NIV

As the dawn gracefully reveals itself, the Holy Spirit awakens me. *"Get out of bed, little one, and come walk with Me"* — an invitation I am delighted to accept. The beauty is breathtaking, and in the stillness of the moment there is only my beloved Lord and me.

Our intimate dance begins. I humbly share my appreciation and worries. *Lord, thank you for being here. My loved ones face many challenges. I am feeling anxious. Please show me how to move through this in a way that brings glory to You. I trust in You.* Then the voice of the Holy Spirit lovingly responds, *"Sweet child, I am so grateful that you honestly and willingly come to Me for guidance. I am here. Breathe. Breathe in My love. Feel My grace shower over you. All is well. My promise is that the challenges are growing each of you — shaping all of you into what I have called you to be. Stop looking at your problems and look at Me and My power. Fix your eyes on Me. For so many years you thought you were the source of your own well-being and theirs. You forgot that I am here. I am your source and also theirs."*

As God's wisdom fills my heart, the emerging day blossoms. The rolling hills glisten with morning dew; the effervescent sun bathes the weeping willows. And the air is infused with the sweet fragrance of magnolias.

Still wrapped in codependent anxiety, I answer, *Lord, I hear You, but I want the pain to stop. I suffer when my family suffers. I want to take their pain away.*

God patiently continues to guide me. *"Little one, who's to say they are suffering when they are going through experiences; this is only your limited perspective. I am using their experiences for their deliverance. My ways are not your ways. Look through My eyes of grace and see that these challenges are growing them and you in character. The*

46

trials give birth to patience, strength, trust, and endurance – My fruit growing in them. Perhaps the most profound gift your trials bring is the desire to share an intimate relationship with Me."

The ruby red cardinals in their splendor grace the vividness of the sapphire sky. Peace begins to soothe my anxious mind as God lovingly continues to speak to my heart. *"Sweet girl, come to Me with all; cast your cares on Me. I am here. When you are scared, come to Me. Pray for My peace to come upon you and those you are worried about. Your prayer is an affirmation of your trust in Me. You are often powerless to change the circumstances of another; you are not God. As you accept this humility, I will empower you by My power and I will guide you. For now the most powerful actions you can take are to pray, love, understand, and encourage others. See your loved ones in My hands and declare by faith My promises over them. All is well. Let go of control, My child, and let Me in. You will be amazed at what I can do."*

As I hear these words, the silence of the dawn is broken open by a thunderous *whoooooossssssshhhh*. Looking up to the heavens, I see not one but five hot air balloons gracing the atmosphere. Fire allows them to rise. Letting go of the tethers frees them, and the skillful navigation of the captain carries them with ease to their destination. This is what unfolds in our lives. Each time I remember to let go and let God – to trust His wisdom, and follow His guidance – the gifts are profound.

When I trust, I see God continuously working in my life and in the lives of my loved ones. So just for today, I am willing to see myself and those I love in God's hands – to take the next right action and walk through this day with His blessed assurance.

Thank you, God, that You are always here. Help me to let go and let You lead.

Grace Lens

After a particularly challenging night, I arose at dawn and prayed for guidance. I asked my beloved Lord to renew my faith and help me see the situation through the eyes of grace.

As I stepped out in the morning air, I noticed the rising sun, glowing with luminosity. To the right of a sunbeam, a skywriter had painted an arc of light. It was beautiful through my human eyes.

Yet when I looked through the lens of my camera, what appeared was astonishing—an angel in a full halo of light. In that moment, wonder eclipsed worry. How different would the circumstances of our lives be if we viewed them through the eyes of grace?

Indeed, when we change the way we look at things, the things we look at change.

Lord, help me to see life through the eyes of grace. For through Your grace lens, oh, the wonders and blessings I receive.

4

God's Power in His Word

Using God's Word to Move through Change

Just as nature provides various seasons, we too experience multiple seasons in our lives. Each season is an integral part of becoming who God created us to be. Some seasons are full of blessings while others present life-altering challenges. The good news is that God and His nourishing Word equip us with what we need to move through every season.

His Word is like the warmth of a down jacket in winter storms, fertile soil to plant seeds in springtime, a cool refreshing pool in the heat of summer, and the bountiful harvest we receive in autumn. God's Word brings comfort, strength, blessing, wisdom, and most of all, peace.

His Word holds great power. When spoken intentionally, aloud, it becomes a living, breathing meditation—food for our souls. Your inner mind and the enemy may tell you that God's Word is not true, yet Proverbs 30:5 and John 17:17 both share that God's Word is true. Luke 1:45 says, "You are blessed because you believed that the Lord would do what he said" (NLT). We are blessed, nurtured, and fed by the Word of God when we believe His promises over our lives.

God knows how much all of us struggle with limiting beliefs, negative perceptions, and lies of the enemy. Each time we speak God's Word aloud, our minds are renewed. Romans 12:2 elaborates: "Be transformed by the renewing of your mind" (NIV).

So ask the Lord to help your unbelief, renew your mind, and give you the mind of Christ—a mind that believes His promises as you meditate on just a small appetizer of His grace-filled assurances. Speak them aloud, for "faith comes by hearing and hearing by the word of God" (Romans 10:17).

- For a moment take a deep breath and simply believe and declare God is near and He is able to do exceedingly, abundantly beyond anything we envision, imagine, or experience (see Jeremiah 23:23; Ephesians 3:20).

- For a moment take a deep breath and simply believe and declare God is our refuge and all is well (see Psalm 46:1; 2 Kings 5:22).

- For a moment take a deep breath and simply believe and declare God restores our souls, and that goodness and mercy will follow you all the days of our lives (see Psalm 23).

- For a moment take a deep breath and simply believe and declare all things are working together for good, and that what is happening to us will turn out for our deliverance (see Romans 8:28; Philippians 1:19).

- For a moment take a deep breath and simply believe and declare the Lord gives us peace, and that we are blessed when we come in and when we go out (see Numbers 6:26; Deuteronomy 28:6).

- For a moment take a deep breath and simply believe and declare God loves us with an everlasting love, and that we are His treasured possession (see Jeremiah 31:3; Deuteronomy 7:6).

- For a moment take a deep breath and simply believe and declare that the blessings of the Lord make us rich and He adds no sorrow (see Proverbs 10:22).

- For a moment take a deep breath and believe and declare His favor is for a lifetime — that we are safe under the shadow of His wings (see Psalm 30:5; 36:7).

You may feel a million miles away from these promises. I have been right where you are. Yet each time I read His Word and declare His promises over my life, it is like watering the seed of God's potential in my life. I look up and create lists of specific scriptures in my areas of struggle. Then I pray, asking the Holy Spirit to help me experience and live out His promises. I read these promises over and over until they are louder than the limiting beliefs in my mind.

According to Dr. Herbert Lockyer, in his book *All the Promises in the Bible*, there are more than 7,487 promises in the holy Word.[4] Astonishing, that as much as you think your struggles are unique to you, the Bible is filled with promises specific for your problem. Dive into the living water and let His grace overtake you and your circumstances. You can find lists of these scriptures on openbible.info and also on my website gracelovewell.org.

Thank you, Father, for Your precious, priceless promises over our lives. Help us live them out to bring glory and honor to You.

Prayer

Imagine that there is a power that knows all, sees all, and loves all—this power is God. The most powerful tool we have to connect with God is prayer. Prayer is a direct line of communication to the creator of the universe. Just as there are numerous types of phones with which to communicate, there are numerous types of prayer. Some are basic and get the job done, while others are filled with major upgrades and increased power.

One form of prayer I particularly love and find highly effective is prayer of petition using God's Word. These power-packed prayers filled with His scriptures are praying His will, for everything in the Bible is God's will. I have found that these prayers help position me to receive, by faith, what God already has prepared. Matthew 21:22 explains it perfectly: "And whatever you ask in prayer, you will receive, if you have faith" (ESV).

Yet God is not a vending machine to go to whenever you need something. God is a good God who loves to guide you, loves to bless you, and loves to be in relationship with you. Take some time to sit in His presence, to be in His Word as you script your own prayer of petition.

Acrostic for Scriptural Prayers of Petition:

TALK

T—tell God how much you love Him. Thank Him for the good that's in your life. Trust Him.

A—ask Him for what you need and ask for guidance for how to move forward in victory in a way that will bring glory and honor to Him, to be blessed and be a blessing.

L—let go and let God—surrender into His hands any worries, unforgiveness, the way you think it should go, unbelief, sin, or shame.

K—keep your eyes on Jesus and off the problem. Keep praising Him and declaring the scriptures relating to your situation (biblegateway.com is one great place to find them) as you wait patiently for His perfect timing.

Template for Prayer

Heavenly Father, Lord Jesus, and Holy Spirit, I love You and I thank You for_____, _____, and _____. Jesus, I trust in You. Lord, my desire is to _____. Guide me. Show me my next right action to move forward in victory, bringing glory and honor to You. I let go of anything that is blocking me and ask for forgiveness for (confess it)_____. *As I let go, I open up to receive and I declare by faith _____* (insert two or three scriptures pertinent to your situation). *I trust that Your blessing is upon me so I can be blessed and be a blessing. Jesus, I trust in You and pray this in Your holy name.*

Any time fear, worry, and/or unbelief creep into your mind and heart, you have this prayer to build your faith. Then, continue to pray it until a miracle happens.

Thank you, God, for the gift of prayer, for Your amazing promises, and the transformational power of Your Word. Help us to use it wisely.

Trust

> Let the morning bring me word of your unfailing love for I
> have put my trust in you.
>
> Show me the way I should go, for to you I entrust my life.
>
> Psalm 143:8, NIV

I love this scripture. It depicts the trust walk we take with our
beloved Lord. This journey happens step-by-step, moment by
moment, and decision by decision. Trusting God is the deepest
and most life-changing part of our faith walk and our life. It is
messy, beautiful, uncomfortable, and awe inspiring. Trust is a
muscle that needs to be developed and draws us closer to God.

Every time we turn our will and our lives over to God and ask
for His guidance to move forward, the spiritual muscles needed to
trust grow stronger. The evidence of our faith is made manifest. Is
working out at the gym comfortable? No. It takes effort and
sometimes hurts. So does letting go and building a trust muscle.
The word *trust* sparks this acrostic:

T — thoroughly

R — ready to

U — use

S — spiritual

T — truths

At times a spiritual truth comes from the still, small voice of the
Holy Spirit. Sometimes it comes through the prayers and
encouragement of others. It can appear through journaling. And
when I open the Bible and ask the Lord to show me what He
wants me to know, that truth is present. Knowing these truths
opens a way to trust God's will and guidance.

So as we walk through the many seasons of our lives, it is wise
to put our trust in the Lord, for as Proverbs 16:20 promises,

"Whoever gives heed to instruction prospers, and blessed is the one who trusts in the LORD" (NIV).

Thank you, Father, for the way You're working in our lives, that all things are working together for good. We trust You, Lord, and we love You.

Who You Really Are

What do you see when you look in the mirror? When you gaze into your eyes, what thoughts come to mind? For many the first thoughts are negative. We see our wounds, scars, and imperfections. We see through our minds, but our minds can be dumping grounds festering with toxic negative thoughts from childhood, the media, the enemy, and the world telling us who we are and how we must be to have love and acceptance.

When God looks at you, He sees His reflection — the miracle He created — the love of His life, His precious child. This paradox of truth of who we are in God and the lie of who we think we are is a battlefield that keeps us from fulfilling our destiny and living the authentic abundant life God plans for us.

Yet we find hope in God's Word. Romans 12:2 shows us a clear path. "Be transformed by the renewing of your mind" (NIV). When we invite God to renew our minds, we embark on a glorious adventure to step into and up to who we truly are. Is this a quick, easy process? Absolutely not. It is a full-on, ongoing, courageous act of love. If you are diligent, one day you will awaken, and the voice of truth as to who you are in Christ will be far louder than the voice of deception.

When I first came to the Lord, I was broken and overwhelmed by suffering. One morning as I cried out to the Lord about all the tragedies, I heard Him whisper, *"That is not who you are. You are victorious, an overcomer."* This encouragement sparked my curiosity, so I googled "who I am in Christ." Some of the scriptures were completely "over my head," while others were super-turbocharged, breathing life into my soul. I spoke them over myself, inserting my name in them, proclaiming the truth of who I am. I personalized the Word as if Christ was speaking directly to me.

I still pray these scriptures and ask God to show me how to experience their promises. For I know every word of scripture is God-breathed — not just a historical account describing God, but

His love letter to us. His holy Bible shows us clearly who we are in Christ and who He is to us.

Day after day I camped out in these promises. I created vision boards with pictures of my family and myself. I sprinkled them with colorful, life-giving scriptures — reminders of who we are in God. I taped them to the bathroom mirror so I could look into my own eyes and speak life. Each time I read the truth, my mind renewed.

Here are a few verses that awaken, enliven, and renew my mind to the truth of who I am. As much as He loves me, He also loves you, so these truths are for you.

- I am safe under the shadow of God's wings (Psalm 57:1).
- I am forgiven (Ephesians 1:7).
- I am blessed coming in and blessed going out (Deuteronomy 28:6).
- God's favor surrounds me like a shield (Psalm 5:12).
- I am loved with an everlasting love (Jeremiah 31:3).
- In Christ I am given exceedingly great and precious promises (2 Peter 1:4).
- I approach God with boldness, freedom, and confidence (Ephesians 3:12).
- I am confident that God will perfect the work He has begun in me (Philippians 1:6).
- I am God's masterpiece created in Christ to do the good work He has planned (Ephesians 2:10).
- I am established and anointed and blessed by God in Christ (2 Corinthians 1:21).
- I am chosen and dearly loved by God (1 Thessalonians 1:4).
- In Christ I have everything I need (2 Peter 1:3).
- I am chosen and appointed by Christ to bear His fruit (John 15:16).
- I grasp how wide and how long, how high, and how deep Christ's love is for me (Ephesians 3:18).

- I am assured that all things work together for good because I love the Lord and am called according to His purpose (Romans 8:28).
- I am complete in Christ (Colossians 2:10).
- I have the mind of Christ (1 Corinthians 2:16).
- I am a precious child of God (1 John 3:1).
- In Christ I am a new creation; the past is over (2 Corinthians 5:17).
- In Christ I am firmly rooted and now being built up in Him (Colossians 2:7).
- My mind and heart are filled with God's peace (Philippians 4:7).
- In Christ I am victorious (1 John 5:4).
- I am chosen and dearly loved (1 John 5:4).
- I have been made alive together with Christ (Ephesians 2:5).
- From the fullness of God's grace, I receive one blessing after another (John 1:16).
- The grace of our Lord is poured out on me (1 Timothy 1:14).
- I am created to live and walk in victory. In Christ I am always led to triumph (2 Corinthians 2:14).
- I go out in joy and I am led in peace (Isaiah 55:12).
- My healing quickly appears (Isaiah 58:8).
- This is the year of the Lord's favor (Isaiah 61:2).
- Instead of shame I receive a double portion (Isaiah 61:7).
- All who see me will acknowledge that the Lord has blessed me (Isaiah 61:9).
- I delight in the Lord and He gives me the desires of my heart (Psalm 37:4).
- God's grace is lavished on me with wisdom and understanding (Ephesians 1:8).
- I am Christ's friend (John 15:15).
- I have not been given a spirit of fear, but of power, love, and self-discipline (2 Timothy 1:7).
- I am born of God and the evil one cannot touch me (1 John 5:18).
- I am holy and blameless (Ephesians 1:4).

- I am adopted as His child (Ephesians 1:5).
- I know there is a purpose for my sufferings (Ephesians 3:13).

Whether you believe these scriptures or not, proudly and boldly speak them out loud, for they are the truth, and little by little, as you begin to believe them, you will begin to experience them. And oh, how you will bring glory to God when you know the truth.

Thank you, Lord, that You see me, know me, and love me. Help me to know and believe the truth of who I am in You.

Stop, Drop, and Pray

In the middle of a challenge there is always a blessing. In the storm, a rainbow. So where is your focus? On the problem or the One whose power is greater than all?

Yesterday, as my mind became undisciplined like an unruly child, I knew I needed to shift my focus and change my perception. This was a God-sized task, and one I knew I could not do alone. The battlefield of my mind required immediate action. I was called to stop, drop, and pray.

As I poured out my heart to God, I was suddenly greeted by a glorious rainbow over my backyard. In an instant, His wonder overtook my worry. Philippians 4:6–9 from the Message says it perfectly: "Don't fret or worry. Instead of worrying, pray. Let petitions and praises shape your worries into prayers, letting God know your concerns. Before you know it, a sense of God's wholeness, everything coming together for good, will come and settle you down. It's wonderful what happens when Christ displaces worry at the center of your life. Summing it all up, friends, I'd say you'll do best by filling your minds and meditating on things true, noble, reputable, authentic, compelling, gracious—the best, not the worst; the beautiful, not the ugly; things to praise, not things to curse. Put into practice what you learned from me, what you heard and saw and realized. Do that, and God, who makes everything work together, will work you into his most excellent harmonies."

Where is your focus today? On the problem? Or on His power?

May our God of all grace renew our minds and bring us the peace that passes all understanding. And as we are so richly blessed, let us be a blessing to others. In Jesus' name.

5

God's Joy in Our Gratitude

Let Wonder Replace Worry

> The gloom of this world is but a shadow. Behind it, yet within reach, is joy. There is a radiance and glory in the darkness, could we but see, and to see, we have only to look. I beseech you to look!
>
> — Fra. Giovanni Giocondo

Whether you are in a season of joy or a season of sorrow, there are miracles available if you ask the Lord to help you see them through eyes of grace. As I arise from my slumber and thank God for the gift of this new day, my mind is drawn to the miracles held in each precious moment:

- That wonder can eclipse worry, that faith can comfort fear, and that God's love changes everything . . . a miracle.
- That a sperm and an egg unite to become a human being . . . a miracle.
- That each sunrise and sunset paints the sky with a palette of extraordinary hues . . . a miracle.
- That whatever you have experienced, you came through it and you are here . . . a miracle.
- That each new season brings new beauty . . . a miracle.

- That the things we each thought would break our heart actually soften it, allowing us to love more fully and compassionately . . . a miracle.
- That flowers come dressed in many colors . . . a miracle.
- That we give our children roots and they grow wings as they become young adults . . . a miracle.
- That we can grow from our experiences rather than just suffering through them . . . a miracle.
- That a butterfly's divine mission is to delight . . . a miracle.
- That we have tears to release sad feelings and make space for more joy . . . a miracle.
- That our body can see, feel, taste, smell, think, walk, talk, heal, and experience well-being . . . a miracle.
- That a rainbow can burst forth from the darkness of a storm . . . a miracle.
- That we are alive and in relationship with a living, loving God who gives us abundant life . . . a miracle.

The ability to see the miracles in life is simply a change in perception. Are you focusing on what's wrong? Or on the One who can bring you miracles? Invite God to show you all the miracles that abound moment by moment when you are fully present. Be in awe and delight as a child in the gifts your heavenly Father brings. "Delight yourself also in the Lord and He shall give you the desires of your heart" (Psalm 37:4, NKJV).

Thank you, Lord, for eyes to see the wonder of this day.

Out of My Mind and into Grace

As I step out of my door, I step out of my mind. The mind can be so full of day-to-day concerns — the ever-pressing need to fix what is problematic, and the desire for situations to be different from what they are. So to find peace, I step out into nature and invite God to show me the gifts that can only be embraced in the present moment. As I walk beneath the canopy of effervescent blue skies, I feel my Beloved's grace bathe me in joy. "God, thank you," I whisper as the gentle cool breeze kisses my skin. It feels as though God is breathing life back into my very being. Each step brings a new delight, a fresh gift from my creator.

The sweet aroma of jasmine infuses the air. The falling flowers let go of their attachment to the trees that held them so lovingly, and the foliage bends gracefully in the wind. Prayer overtakes the moment. *Lord, I am willing to learn this level of trust, to fill ever-waking moments with Your sweetness and beauty. I am willing to learn to let go of control and let You lead me. I am willing to be flexible and graceful as the winds of change blow through my life. Please lead the way.*

Wonder abounds as an entourage of dragonflies and butterflies escorts me, dancing joyfully through the air. God is not nature; yet everything I witness is God's creation — my Beloved's gift to me when I am fully present and open to receive. "Every good gift and every perfect gift is from above, and comes down from the Father of lights" (James 1:17, NKJV).

As I walk through this moment, through this day, awareness arises. How many gifts have I missed as a result of being preoccupied with the past, a problem, or the future? What about the moments of pain, sadness, and fear? Could these also hold gifts? If I ask God to help me embrace and accept His will and everything that arises from it; if I ask my Beloved to carry me through the valleys I experience; if a knowing then springs forth that I am so profoundly loved that everything I experience is for my good, my growth, and His glory, who am I to judge what is a gift and what is not?

63

From my own human perspective, I can only see a tiny glimpse of reality. For now, I trust deeply and allow God's grace to permeate my being. If I could see through His eyes, I would know that all is well, that He is my well—and that I can be filled with grace at any moment I remember to go to my heavenly Father.

To experience the fullness of this grace, I will make mistakes, feel emotions, make progress, face challenges, and have opportunities to grow. Then I will step out of my head back to the embrace of Christ. For my beloved creator is ever-present, waiting with open arms to lead me, renew me, walk beside me, and show me my next step. By His grace I discover gifts, receive the blessings, and give thanks for the aliveness of this human experience. In my humanness I have the glorious opportunity to witness God's beauty in the present moment.

Thank you, God, for the gift of grace, the beauty of nature, and the ability to be fully alive to experience it.

Gratitude in the Middle of It

Gratitude is my lifeline, a moment-by-moment infusion of grace. It is a daily practice—one that transforms my life one moment at a time. But how do you give thanks when you're in the middle of change, in the middle of grief, in the middle of a challenge? This is when the practice becomes most profound.

Seventeen years ago my sister-in-law was dying of cancer, my baby was critically ill in the hospital, and I was physically and emotionally exhausted. I called a friend and poured out my heart, detailing all the suffering we were experiencing.

She calmly responded, "You need to write a gratitude list."

I was angry. "There's nothing to be grateful for."

She encouraged me to write ten things I was thankful for—to sit there until I was finished.

It took me two hours to think of ten things for which I was grateful. They were ordinary things including having a house, food on the table, the blessing of my children. A bit of peace washed over me.

The next day I again wrote the things I was grateful for. This time it took me ten minutes to think of ten things.

By the third day, my life force was renewed, so I chose to write down a hundred things. My circumstances had not changed, yet the eyes through which I chose to see my life did. I still had moments of grief and sadness, yet by intentionally looking for what was working, I found peace right in the middle of my challenges.

Over the years, as I continued my daily gratitude practice, I became aware of many blessings. A newfound joy arose—a joy not dependent on my life circumstances. Then several years ago, when our family was challenged again in ways we never imagined, I was led to a miraculous book that changed my life: *One Thousand Gifts* by Ann Voskamp. Ann details her gratitude journey in the messiness of life and talks about consecutively numbering her gratitude journal. She encourages readers to look for the gift in each moment, even during the painful experiences. She enlightens readers by reminding us that each time we find something to be grateful for, we also discover an additional way that God loves us.[5]

So in the middle of our deepest, darkest night—in a season of profound pain—I began at number one. Each night I numbered the things I was grateful for. Some nights it was five things and other nights twenty or more. I experienced God's love.

Today God has shown me His love in more than thirty thousand ways. As I view my life through the eyes of gratitude, I realize many of those painful life experiences have been transformed and God has brought blessings out of them. Are there still challenges? Of course. But each is an opportunity to draw nearer to God and grow in character.

What was most profound was to examine the two major challenges our family faced in comparison to the thousands of gifts I had expressed. As I right-sized the problems, the magnitude of God's majesty multiplied and magnified.

By simply pausing for a moment and acknowledging something we are grateful for, our hope and clarity are restored. Gratitude moments can be spent appreciating the beauty in nature, what works in our bodies, and the love in our relationships.

We can give thanks in the challenges, for the tears that cleanse our souls, for how we have grown through them, for what we have learned, for how resilient we are, and for how God carried us when we were too broken to move forward.

And then there are the most delicious moments of all—having full sensory gratitude for what we see, smell, taste, hear, feel, and experience in the present moment. For in this moment, God dwells.

Today I give thanks for an ever-present God in our very human experience.

May you experience the fullness of God's love and blessings as you begin to view your life through the lens of gratitude.

6

God's Hand in the Miraculous

Miracles on Facebook

There are moments when the magnitude of His mercy meets the magnitude of our human experience — when ten years of praying turns into a "suddenly" experience of breakthrough.

For many years I've wrestled with numerous health challenges. I've had times of well-being and other moments when my health created life-changing limitations for our family and me. I've tried everything from traditional medicine to holistic care. In my journey, I learned to rely on the Lord for everything.

As my body weakened, by God's grace, His Spirit within me became more alive. I spent hours in the Word — studying, meditating on, praying, and proclaiming His promises of well-being. God was faithful in the middle of the challenge, giving me strength, wisdom, love, and a very patient husband.

The sequence of events that followed was so profound that even as a writer I could not script a greater tale. Every word is as it happened.

69

In October 2014 my health took a turn for the worse. After running numerous tests, the doctors were as perplexed as they had been in the past as to my autoimmune challenges. We had many prayer warriors praying for my well-being. The Holy Spirit alive within me for years had promised well-being, yet my physical body had yet to receive that memo. During this time I regularly cried out to the Lord for guidance, and many times He would epically show off in supernatural signs and wonders.

One particular autumn day, as I drove home from Bible study, the Lord outdid Himself. With worship music on the radio, the presence of God overtook me, and I prayed a prayer of deep surrender about my health. A moment later, I pulled up behind a truck bearing the sign "Well done." I laughed the whole way home. Later in the day I was feeling anxious as I drove to a doctor's appointment, so I prayed for God to show me He was with me. I know He always is, yet I often need reminders. I was overjoyed to see three trucks with the logo "Around the Clock," reminding me again of God's constant presence. A wave of peace trumped my anxious mind.

As I sat in the doctor's office seeking a second opinion for a new treatment, I glanced at the test results from my previous physician. I had reviewed these test results many times but never noticed — in the doctor's scribble next to several of my immune markers — "God, God."

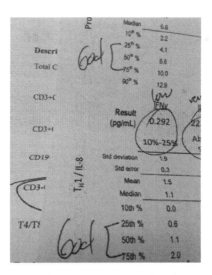

Amazed, I sat in awestruck wonder. I was perplexed at the ways God was revealing His presence to me that day. When I discussed a new treatment option with the physician, he was adamantly opposed to it. I smiled, sensing I was embarking on a supernatural journey held in the assurance of God's grace and mercy.

As I returned home buzzing with joy at the undeniable God kisses that I had just experienced, I opened a piece of mail and dropped to my knees weeping. The letter was from my church and shared how the executive pastors had prayed and fasted for a week for my family. This act of love was even more profound, for we are part of a large megachurch. The power in others' praying and fasting on my behalf was bearing fruit in the supernatural ways I saw God's presence.

For the first time I began to believe what the Holy Spirit had told me about my health—that I would be well. Day after day I asked the Lord to help me experience the truth of His Word. Some of my favorite scriptures to declare are: (1) Acts 3:16, that by the power of His name I am made strong and given perfect health; (2) Jeremiah 33:6, that the Lord brings health and healing and I enjoy peace and security; and (3) Mark 5:34: "Daughter, your faith has made you well, go in peace and be healed of your disease."

Day by day the voice of truth, the voice of faith, became louder than the voice of fear. In the turbulence of my mind I was fighting the good fight of faith. Yet my body was growing weaker.

Several months went by and then the windows of heaven opened in ways I have never seen. I received a settlement letter in the mail from an airline carrier regarding a concussion I had experienced on a flight home from Alaska. That injury left me even weaker than before. We had no intention of suing, however, the airline wanted to compensate me for the injury. In my heart I heard the Holy Spirit ask me to write a letter to the flight attendant who caused the concussion, to let her know I forgave her and that I was completely healed. Needless to say I was beyond perplexed — I was not completely healed; in fact I was weaker than ever. So I asked the Lord again how to move forward. He guided me to do the GRACE process of forgiveness that I shared earlier in this book. So I sat down and poured my heart out to the Lord with the intention of moving forward in full forgiveness. I felt the heavy burden of hidden resentment melt away.

Then I prayed, "Father, if You want me to write this letter and tell her I am completely well, You have to write the letter for me, because if I write it, I will be lying." The words flowed onto the page. I wept as I mailed it. Little did I know that I was not only walking by faith but I was calling things which were not as though they were (see Romans 4:17, KJV). By walking in obedience and forgiveness, I was opening a way for the miraculous to unfold.

The next day I hit another breaking point; my human strength could bear no more. I dropped to my knees in utter desperation and cried out to the Lord, "Father, if there is a way for me to get healthy, Lord, please show me now. I cannot do this anymore. I surrender all of it. Jesus, I trust in You."

Like any good Christian, I got off my knees and got on Facebook. A friend from high school had posted an article by broadcaster Glenn Beck. The Holy Spirit prompted me to open it. In the article, Beck shared his many years of significant health issues. Doctors finally discovered that he had a brain injury.[6]

The article went on to share about Beck's amazing recovery at a brain treatment center. Ten years previously, right before my health challenges began, I too had a serious concussion in a severe car accident. I'd also had several others as a child and an adult.

I immediately browsed the website of this treatment center and found many of their past patients telling my story.

So, me of little faith called out to God again, "Father, if this is where You want me to go, please give me a sign." At that moment, the postman delivered a package from Amazon—a book I had ordered. Who had endorsed the book? Glenn Beck.

Laughing at the goodness of God, I returned to the treatment center's website and noticed that the director was both a neurologist and a chiropractor. So I called my chiropractor in Florida and asked him if he knew of this doctor who practiced in Atlanta and Dallas.

He responded, "The man is a genius, and my best friend is this doctor's best friend. It takes forever to get into the clinic, but maybe my friend can get you in." Now the tears were rolling down my face as God was truly directing and ordering my steps perfectly.

The next day the clinic called to offer me an appointment. They told me I was either so blessed or so loved or all of the above, because three people had called them to ensure that they got me in quickly — which they did — the following week.

As I approached the entrance to the Carrick Brain Center, the miracles continued. Above the building, a sky writer had drawn five crosses. I smiled and thanked God for this priceless opportunity He had given me. Greeted with joy and loving hugs from the doctors who were about to change my life, we quickly began the evaluation. After hours of intensive testing, Dr. Traster, in his beautiful, soft-spoken way, smiled and proudly proclaimed that he discovered the root cause of my health challenges and could fix it!

The team began moving my head, neck, and eyes in various positions to remedy the damage from the head injury.

When I got to the clinic, my balance was at 0 percent with my head turned or eyes closed. My eyes would cross, sending my body into shock. I could barely walk without holding on to the wall, and I could not walk up more than two steps. After the treatment my balance increased to 90 percent, and I was able to run down the hallway and easily climb a flight of steps. Remarkable results unfolded. So much so that one of the doctors burst into tears and asked me to pray for her. God was not only glorified in the healing, but as I shared the supernatural way God led me to Carrick and the astonishing results that were unfolding, the doctors' faith expanded, as they shared they were watching a miracle unfold before their eyes.

The doctors told me that the level of brain impairment I had and the level of well-being I now have is simply miraculous. Developmental vision issues I've had since I was a baby are almost gone. The autoimmune disease is in remission. My nervous system functioning is greatly improved and my balance is normal. There are still issues to tweak. However, according to them, my brain is completely "new." I have my life back. I do home brain-based exercises several times a day to maintain my progress and occasionally have follow-up visits with the doctor. I praise God for this mighty miracle.

During that long season, ten years since the accident and devastating health challenges, I received the greatest gift of all. I came to know and trust that our God is healer, comforter, the great physician, redeemer, sustainer, and deliverer. I realize now I can also experience His goodness and love in the joy of life. I got to know Him in pain, and now I simply love being in His presence and being of service. He is a God who since the beginning of time has performed miracles, and He still performs miracles today. I praise Him.

Wherever you find yourself today, don't give up hope. In a nanosecond God can change everything. The season you're in can give birth to miracles. Isaiah 43:18–19 states it beautifully: "Forget the former things; do not dwell on the past. See, I am doing a new thing! Now it springs up; do you not perceive it?" (NIV).

Acts 10:34 proclaims, "God is no respecter of persons" (KJV). As I said in the beginning, the same God who did this for me can do it for you. Let my testimony of the Lord's miraculous power expand your vision of what is possible. And as Matthew 19:26 declares, "With God all things are possible" (KJV).

God is so good, and He showed me that no matter what we experience, He is so alive and in control. Our part is to cry out, surrender, be obedient, and trust Him.

Indeed, God makes all things new. I'm in awe of His signs and wonders, and most of all, His unending love.

God is alive on Facebook. He is alive everywhere. Keep posting, encouraging, and praying for one another.

May the God of all grace show His miraculous power in each of your lives. And from the fullness of His grace may each of you and your loved ones receive one blessing after another. In Jesus' name.

God Is in Control

The miracles began as we boarded the plane for my second round of treatment. My friend and I were separated by several rows. I asked God to use me wherever He would have me sit. I sat down next to a young man who shared that he'd just lost his job and was terribly depressed. When I asked if I could pray for him, he burst into tears as we took His sorrow to the Lord in prayer. As he thanked me, another young man sat down between us. We began to talk, and for the next two hours discussed the goodness of God, the power of the Bible, and the miracles that have unfolded in both of our lives. The first passenger overheard me share about healing from the brain injury. Suddenly his eyes lit up as he shared how he also had a severe head trauma. God so perfectly positioned me to share my journey of miraculous healing.

As good as that was, God was not done yet. There was severe weather over Atlanta, so we had to circle several times because visibility was low. The plane began running out of gas, so we had to stop in Macon to refuel. As passengers heard this news, several began to cry, curse, and become angry at the thought of missing their connections. The young man next to me and I began to quietly pray that God would use this delay for His purpose and that we could trust that He was in control. Within moments God's peace came over the cabin—a peace that passes all understanding. After an hour and a half delay on the ground, we headed back to Atlanta.

As we made our ascent through the dense fog and darkness of the storm, we broke through to the most glorious light. The clouds were imbued with orange, violet, magenta, and robin's-egg blue from the setting sun. The full moon rose above God's glorious colors. To my delight, jet trails had drawn a cross under the moon. If not for the delay, we would have missed that magnificence. And if that was not enough, as we landed, the pilot announced that all connecting flights were waiting for the passengers on our plane.

Awed by God's goodness, I realized once again that in our human minds we never know why things don't go our way, yet when we trust that God is in control, lean into His goodness, and ask how we can be of service, then, as Romans 8:26–28 says, "Meanwhile, the moment we get tired in the waiting, God's Spirit is right alongside helping us along. If we don't know how or what to pray, it doesn't matter. He does our praying in and for us, making prayer out of our wordless sighs, our aching groans. He knows us far better than we know ourselves, knows our pregnant condition, and keeps us present before God. That's why we can be so sure that every detail in our lives of love for God is worked into something good" (MSG).

Thank you, Lord, that You use all things together for our good.

Miracles

Once again miracles began as the plane ascended toward the clouds. I prayed I would be blessed and be a blessing as I embarked on my third round of brain treatments. The first blessing I witnessed was the dark of night being broken open by the most glorious sunrise.

Totally fatigued from my teenage child's challenging growth experiences and the upcoming medical treatments, I truly wanted to sleep on the plane and be left alone. Fortunately, God had a different plan. The woman next to me politely began airplane small talk. The conversation quickly turned to faith, and I began to share the miracle healing I was experiencing. Her eyes lit up as she shared that her husband and daughter had also been impacted by traumatic brain injury. So for the second time in three trips to the Carrick Brain Center, God placed me next to people who needed to hear my story. For the next two hours we prayed for each other and spoke about God's goodness in the middle of trials and joy. Blessed and blessing number two.

After landing, I received blessing number three when I was greeted by the most adorable eighteen-year-old who helped me with my bags. When I asked him how he was doing, he smiled and proudly proclaimed that he was so blessed because God woke him up.

Blessed and blessing number four: a wonderful driver picked me up to take me to the clinic. Our small talk turned to our teenagers. For the next hour we encouraged one another and prayed for each other's children.

Blessed and blessing number five: when I arrived at the hotel, I was greeted by an amazing doorman who was also a pastor. He had prayed for me on all my visits. With arms wide open he greeted me with love. Once again he prayed for me. As I shared the amazing grace God was pouring into me, his eyes lit up. He said he was preaching a message on grace that weekend and would be using my testimony to encourage others.

All of this happened before 8:00 in the morning! Dear ones, if you are willing to let the Lord bless you to be a blessing, you will embark on an amazing God adventure filled with meaning and purpose. Buckle your seatbelts; it's a glorious ride.

Thank you, God, for divine appointments and answered prayers. I am grateful for the trials that allow me to experience Your awestruck wonder.

Just the Beginning

Although this is the end of this book, our connection with God and living an abundant life in Christ is an ongoing process. It is my deepest prayer that you feel God's love as you have never felt it before. I have seen so many prayers answered. Others I am still waiting on the Lord to answer in His time, in His way. Yet as I wait, I have the greatest gift of all — an intimate connection with the God of grace amazing, love consuming, and joy abounding. He is there for you too — in the middle of the night, at the break of dawn, in the depth of challenge, and in the joy of blessing. He is alive and waiting for you with open arms. The only way to know Him is to be in His Word and in His presence. Regardless of your circumstances, He is the answer.

In your weakness God is strength.
In your sadness God is comfort.
In your illness God is healer.
In your lack God is provider.
In your confusion God is all-knowing.
In your not enough God is more than enough.
In your bondage God is freedom.
In your burden God is burden bearer.
In your worry God is peace.
In your failure God is victory.

As you let go of the magnitude of your problem and fall into the majesty of His mercy, you will begin to see a multidimensional, all-knowing, all-powerful God. The creator God who breathed and the stars came to be (Psalm 33:6) is the same God who knows you so intimately that He knows the number of hairs on your head (Luke 12:7). Cry out to Him, get in a Bible-based church, dive into His Word, and God will amaze your human experience.

You may not understand what you are going through, but it is no surprise to God. Place it all in His hands of grace. Ask Him to guide you. You'll get through it. I am praying for you and believing for His miracles in your life. God is here. You are loved. All is well.

> *Dear God,*
>
> *You are the creator of the universe who is as close as our breath. I thank you, Father, that we can come boldly to Your throne of grace where we can cast our cares upon You because You care so fully for us. So many are in need of Your blessing, mercy, lovingkindness, healing, and most of all, Your love. So I ask that You cover us and our loved ones in Your amazing grace, shower us in Your peace that passes all understanding, and show us how to move through the joys and challenges of life in a way that glorifies You. We surrender all to You, Lord. As we are so richly blessed, let us be a blessing for others. In Jesus' name.*

Digging Deeper for Group or Individual Study

For me, reading a book is wonderful. My experiences are validated, I gain insight into how the author moved through his or her challenges, and many times I reap nuggets of wisdom. Yet sadly, if I don't put into practice what I read, I rarely see a lasting impact in my life.

For this reason I designed a six-week Bible study for *Overtaken by Grace*. It is filled with experiential activities, life-giving scriptures, and questions for reflection to deepen your walk with the Lord. This Bible study can either be done in a group format, with a prayer partner, or on your own.

My deepest prayer for each of you is that the time you invest in studying and applying these principles leads to a deeper, more love-infused relationship with the Lord. And as you are so richly blessed, I know beyond a shadow of a doubt that you will be a blessing to others. In Jesus' name.

Let your adventure begin.

Chapter 1

God's Presence in Our Lives

Opening Prayer

Heavenly Father, Lord Jesus, Holy Spirit, what an honor to gather together in Your presence. Lord, reveal yourself to our hearts, minds, and souls. Holy Spirit, come into this study in a way that glorifies You. Touch us all in a supernatural way that we may be blessed to be a blessing. In Jesus' name.

Introduction

Wouldn't it be amazing if in this human walk called life we found the perfect partner who always loves us, always forgives us, always comforts us, and in the valley always leads us to victory? Wouldn't you want to spend time and invest in this relationship? That perfect partner is here — our heavenly Father, Lord Jesus, and His Holy Spirit. We have been given the great honor and privilege to have access to the King of kings and the Lord of lords. So now let's spend some time getting to know Him in a deeper, more intimate way.

Activity

This activity will enable the group to collectively experience the presence of God.

Play a worship song about God's greatness and majesty. (Some options: "How Great Is Our God" by Chris Tomlin; "Awesome God" by Michael W. Smith.)

Have members close their eyes and breathe deeply as they listen, allowing themselves to be washed in God's loving presence. After the song, have each member declare out loud who God is, praising His greatness, might, and power.

Read the following scriptures about God's character and attributes. (Before the group meeting, you may wish to write each of these references on a separate piece of paper in order to pass them out among the group members.)

> 1 John 4:8, Genesis 1:1, Isaiah 9:6, Revelation 1:8, Exodus 6:3, John 1:1, Exodus 17:15, Genesis 17:1, Psalm 103:1–3, John 10:11, Jeremiah 23:6, Isaiah 40:28, Isaiah 12:2, Revelation 19:16, Colossians 1:17, Isaiah 44:6

Questions for Reflection

1. How did you feel being still in God's presence?

2. After reading the introduction and chapter 1, did you have any insight into the power of God in your own life?

3. When you look at the magnitude of who God is in relationship to the challenges you face, what practices can you put in place to help you know Him more and trust Him more?

4. What blocks you from spending time with the Lord?

Homework

1. Write down any challenges you are facing now. Whatever trial you face, write next to it the aspect of God that covers your particular challenge. Then look up scriptures on who God is in that challenge. Declare those promises out loud until you begin to believe them.

2. Read chapter 2 and be prepared to discuss what you have learned.

Closing Prayer

Father God, Lord Jesus, and Holy Spirit, thank you for this time together. Thank you for the magnitude of Your majesty. Lord, we declare by faith that each of us and our loved ones know Your goodness, mercy, love, favor, blessing, peace, and well-being. Guide us all, bless us to be a blessing, and may we bring glory and honor to You. In Jesus' name.

Chapter 2

God's Love in Our Relationships

Opening Prayer

Father God, Lord Jesus, Holy Spirit, thank you for Your power and Your presence. Lord, we trust You with this study and we place it into Your hands. We trust You with our relationship to You, with ourselves, and with each other. Reveal Your truth to our hearts so we can love as You love. Speak through Your Word and through each of us, that we may be blessed to be a blessing. In Jesus' name.

Introduction

Perhaps the most joyful and challenging part of life is our relationships with ourselves and with each other. God is our source of all love, all forgiveness, and all mercy, and with these things in place our relationships will flourish. Yet in our humanness we have resentments, unforgiveness, and judgment. Let's dive in and look at God's power in our relationships.

Activity (materials needed: a small bag of rocks)

Ask for a volunteer and have him or her open up both hands. Then have the members each say something that frustrates them in their relationships. Continue going around the group as you do the following activity. As each member shares a sentence about something that frustrates or angers them, place a rock in the volunteer's hands. Continue around the group again and again, placing rocks for each comment made.

As the volunteer's hands fill up, ask how it feels. Acknowledge that it hurts and is heavy. Share with the group this is what it feels like to carry the weight of unforgiveness, resentments, and judgment.

Ask the group, "If your hands were so full of problems, would you be able to hold on to God and your loved ones, or receive any blessing?"

Now ask the group members if they are willing to give to God all of the burdens, forgive the resentments, and release the judgment. With each thing the group members are willing to let go, have the volunteer put a rock back in the bag until all the rocks are gone.

Now ask, "With your hands empty, which feels better? Which way would enable you to love as God loves and receive His blessing?"

Scripture

Read the following scriptures about God's love and forgiveness in our relationships. (Before the group meeting, you may wish to write each of these references on a separate piece of paper in order to pass them out among the group members.)

> John 13:34, 1 Corinthians 13:4–8, 1 Peter 4:8, 1 John 4:18–19, Hebrews 10:24, Colossians 3:14, Ephesians 4:2, Matthew 22:37–39, Ephesians 4:32, Luke 6:37, Luke 23:34

Questions for Reflection

1. What insights did you gain from the rock activity?

2. After reading chapter 2, what insights did you gain that would help you in your own relationships?

3. Is there anyone you need to forgive?

4. Think of a time when you forgave someone. What changed in you? What changed in your relationship? Did any blessings come from that?

5. Was there a particular scripture that stood out for you and how can you apply that to your life?

Homework

1. Spend some quiet time with the Lord asking Him to search your heart if there's anything that you need to forgive or anything you need to let go of. Then apply what you learned this week to your personal circumstance.

2. Read chapter 3 and be prepared to discuss what you have learned.

Closing Prayer

Father, in the name of Jesus, I thank you, Lord, that we love because You first loved us. We thank you for the families and friends You have blessed us with. Holy Spirit, fill us with Your divine love so we can love as You love. We love You, Lord, and we trust You and pray this in Your holy name.

Chapter 3

God's Peace in Our Emotions

Opening Prayer

Oh Lord Jesus, heavenly Father, and Holy Spirit, we lift Your name on high. We praise You for Your power and Your presence. Lord, we surrender this study into Your hands. Let Your Word and Your Holy Spirit come alive in and through each of us. We are open to receive and to be blessed and transformed, bringing glory and honor to You. We love You, Lord, and we pray this in Jesus' name.

Introduction

Psalm 139 teaches us that we are fearfully and wonderfully made. God designed every bit of us, including our emotions. Yet though the Lord gave us very human feelings, if not managed effectively, acting on them can cause chaos in our lives. The good news is we can use our emotions to draw nearer to God and to experience more of His peace.

Activity Number 1 (materials needed: one balloon)

Hold the balloon up and explain to the group that this is your mind and your body. Ask the group to start calling out things that make them sad, afraid, or worried. With each comment, blow up the balloon until it's just about ready to burst. Then ask the group what would happen if one more thing made you sad or worried?

Now let go of some of the air. Ask, "Would you have more capacity to deal effectively with your life if you let things go? How different would your day go if you emptied out your heart to the Lord first thing in the morning?" Say, "We have this opportunity to let go of stress as we surrender our cares, worries, fears, doubts, and unbelief to the Lord."

Activity Number 2 (materials needed: small pieces of paper and pens)

Pass out pieces of paper and pens. Ask each member to write down anything that is disturbing their peace. Collect these papers and throw them in the trash. Explain that this is one way to let go.

Once the group has let go of their worries, explain to them that now they can be filled with God's promises and replace their worries with His Word. Say, "God's Word soothes comforts and brings peace." As a group, have each individual read one of the scriptures below, and as they hear them, ask the group members to breathe deeply and receive each one as if the Lord was speaking directly to them.

Scriptures

Read the following scriptures about finding peace. (Before the group meeting, you may wish to write each of these references on a separate piece of paper in order to pass them out among the group members.)

> Romans 1:6–7, Romans 2:10, Romans 8:6, Romans 15:13, Romans 15:33, Romans 16:20, 1 Corinthians 1:3, 2 Corinthians 1:2, Ephesians 4:3, Galatians 5:22, Galatians 6:16, Ephesians 1:2, Ephesians 6:23, Philippians 1:2, Colossians 1:2, 1 Thessalonians 1:1, 2 Thessalonians 1:2, Titus 1:4, 2 Peter 1:2, 2 John 1:3, Jude 1:2, Revelation 1:4

Questions for Reflection

1. What came to mind for you as you witnessed the balloon activity?

2. What insights did you gain from reading chapter 3 that you can apply to your own life?

3. What blocks your peace? What actions can you take to let go of whatever blocks God's peace in your life?

4. Did you notice any patterns in the scriptures? How did you feel after hearing and reading what God's Word tells us about peace?

5. What is one action you can take this week to experience more of God's peace?

Homework

1. Write a letter to God each morning, pouring out your heart and asking for His wisdom and peace.

2. Read chapter 4 and be prepared to discuss what you have learned.

Closing Prayer

Father God, Jesus, and Holy Spirit, thank you that You are the prince of peace, and that as we cast our cares upon You, You give us the peace that passes all understanding. Thank you, Lord, that You are always here guiding and blessing each of us and our loved ones. We give You all honor, glory, and praise. In Jesus' name.

Chapter 4

God's Power in His Word

Opening Prayer

Heavenly Father, Lord Jesus, Holy Spirit, we praise You for Your power, Your presence, and Your unfailing love. Thank you, Lord, that we can gather together to come into a deeper relationship with You as we sit and absorb your Word. Holy Spirit, touch each person here, giving them a fresh revelation of who You are. Touch them, Lord, with Your supernatural grace. Lord, help us to speak only what is from You, and let us have ears to hear Your truth. We thank you, Lord, and we pray this in Your holy name.

Introduction

Second Timothy 3:16 says every word of scripture is God-breathed, His love letter to us, our instruction manual on how to live a good life. Whether you are new in your faith walk or have been walking with the Lord for many years, the foundation of our faith and living the fullest, most abundant life comes from knowing who we are in Christ. His Word molds us, shapes us, and guides us. The words we speak deeply impact ourselves and each other.

Activity (materials needed: a handheld mirror, a computer open to the website www.masaru-emoto.net/English/wter-crystal.html, showing photos from The Hidden Messages in Water, if possible)

Pass the mirror around and have each member of the group look at him or herself. Then ask, "What do you see? How many of you saw flaws or judged yourself? Did anyone see anything good?"

Read the following to the group:

> Dr. Masaru Emoto, a Japanese scientist, wanted to study the impact of our words on our physical environment. In his experiment he labeled vials of water with words that described either affirming or derogatory sentiments, such as: "You fool," "You disgust me," "Love and gratitude," "Thank you," and "Peace." He spoke each of these phrases over the corresponding water samples and then froze them.
>
> He designed a special procedure using an electron microscope to see the water crystals that formed from the samples. His results were astonishing. In the water samples that were spoken and labeled with derogatory terms, the water crystals looked chaotic. The samples that were labeled with affirming words formed beautiful crystalline structures.
>
> He illustrates these studies in his book The Hidden Messages in Water.[7] You can also find photos of these experiments on his website.[8] [Show the group the website photos if available, http://www.masaru-emoto.net/english/water-crystal.html]
>
> One of the observations Dr. Emoto made after this experiment was that the majority of our bodies are made up of water. He believes that our words impact our physical bodies.
>
> A wonderful scripture exemplifies this: "Death and life are in the power of the tongue" (Proverbs 18:21, AMP).
>
> As we speak God's Word over ourselves and those we love, we speak life.

Explain to the group that each of us is God's beautiful creation, and when we judge or criticize ourselves, we are criticizing what God made.

Scriptures

Have group members read the following scriptures about God's Word and how God views us. (Before the group meeting, you may wish to write each of these references on a separate piece of paper in order to pass them out among the group members.)

> Psalm 57:1, Ephesians 1:7, Deuteronomy 28:6, Psalm 5:12, Jeremiah 31:3, Ephesians 3:12, Ephesians 2:10, 2 Corinthian 1:21, 1 Thessalonians 1:4, 2 Peter 1:3, 2 Corinthians 5:17 Philippians 4:7, Ephesians 2:10 (MSG), 1 John 5:4, 1 Timothy 1:14, Isaiah 58:8, Ephesians 3:13

Pair up each group member with a partner and have each take turns saying out loud, "I am _____ in Christ. You are _____ in Christ."

Questions for Reflection

1. What felt different when you looked in the mirror before knowing who you are in Christ and after?

2. What insights did you gain from chapter 4 that you can apply to your own life?

3. How would your life change if you started to deeply believe and truly know who you are in Christ?

4. Does anyone have any creative ideas that would help you remember, on a daily basis, who you are?

Homework

1. Pick out four scriptures that especially resonate with you. Read them aloud to yourself in the mirror.

2. Make note in your journal of any changes in your mood, outlook, or life.

3. Read chapter 5 and be prepared to discuss what you have learned.

Closing Prayer

Thank you, Lord, for the time together, for Your Word that shows us who we are. Lord, search our hearts and renew our minds to the truth of who we are in You, for when we know the truth, the truth will set us free to fulfill the divine destiny You have placed within us. Lord, we love You and we pray this in Your holy name.

Chapter 5

God's Joy in Our Gratitude

Opening Prayer

Heavenly Father, Lord Jesus, we come to You so grateful for Your love, for Your Word, and for Your presence in our lives. Lord, we surrender this study into Your hands. Give us wisdom, Lord, and let Your Holy Spirit speak through Your Word so we can continue to grow into the people You've called us to be. We pray this in Jesus' name.

Introduction

Gratitude, the sweet nectar of life, is being aware of the way the Lord blesses us, both in the joys and challenges. Gratitude is a discipline, a practice that leads to a greater intimacy with God, enhanced well-being, and increased joy. So let's dive into the study of gratitude.

Activity (materials needed: enough blueberries for the group to have two each)

Pass out the blueberries and invite each group member to take two. Instruct each person to eat one of them. Then have several people share what they experienced, what it tasted like, and what they noticed about it. Now invite the members to place the other blueberry in their mouth but not eat it. Have them take their time to feel it, to smell it, and to experience it. Have them think about how it was grown and all the people needed to bring it to market. Then invite the group to slowly eat it.

Now have the group share the difference between both experiences.

Share the following thought: By slowing down, our capacity to notice details, to be present, and to experience gratitude increased.

It is true in every area of our lives, our relationships, and our intimacy with God. Each moment of life is filled with things to be grateful for: colors, shapes, sensation, smells, faces, people, love, wisdom, the material, the natural, relationships, our bodies, and our minds. As you begin to look at things to be grateful for, you become a hunter for joy on an amazing God adventure. The more you look for things to be grateful for, the more you find.

Scriptures

Have group members read the following scriptures about gratitude. (Before the group meeting, you may wish to write each of these references on a separate piece of paper in order to pass them out among the group members.)

> Psalm 136:1, James 1:17, Hebrews 12:28, Colossians 3:15, Psalm 107:1, Psalm 50:23, Psalm 100:1–5, Acts 24:3, 2 Corinthians 2:14, Philippians 4:6–8, 1 Thessalonians 5:16–18

After reading the scriptures, spend a few minutes going on a "rampage of gratitude." Have each member call out things they're grateful for and thank God for them.

Questions for Reflection

1. What insights did you take away from chapter 5?

2. How different did you feel being present and thanking God for the blessings in your life?

3. What is something beautiful that came out of a challenge for which you can be thankful?

4. How can you incorporate gratitude into your life on a daily basis?

Homework

1. Go on your own gratitude hunt, writing down each day the things that you're grateful for. Begin to notice how different you feel when you're practicing gratitude.

2. Read chapter 6 and be prepared to discuss what you have learned.

Closing Prayer

Oh thank you, Lord, for the many ways You show us Your love, Your blessings, and Your majesty. Lord, we know it is Your will for us to be grateful in all things. Help us to do that, to see the world, those we love, and ourselves through the eyes of gratitude. We thank you, Lord, and we humbly ask that You pour out Your blessings upon each of us and our loved ones. In Jesus' name.

Chapter 6

God's Hand in the Miraculous

Opening Prayer

Heavenly Father, Lord Jesus, and Holy Spirit, we come to You with so much gratitude for Your love and Your presence in our lives. Lord, we offer this study up to you. Speak to and through each of us through Your Word and Your Holy Spirit. Pour into us in a supernatural way. We thank You and praise You. In Jesus' name we pray.

Introduction

Our God is a God of the miraculous. Our Lord can take the impossible and make it possible. We serve a God who hears our prayers and then in His time and His way answers them. Our job is to ask, surrender, stand faithfully, and wait patiently on His promises.

Scriptures

Invite the group to dive into God's Word by reading the following scriptures as a group. (Before the group meeting, you may wish to write each of these references on a separate piece of paper in order to pass them out among the group members.)

> Matthew 7:7–8, Mark 11:24, Matthew 21:22, John 14:13–14, Jeremiah 33:3, 1 John 5:14–15, Psalm 50:15, John 15:7, Hebrews 4:15, Psalm 103:1–22, Ephesians 3:20

Activity (materials needed: enough paper and pens for the group)

This activity will encourage each group member to script their own biblical prayer to God. Have each person look up any scriptures they find either on Google or in the back of their Bibles that relate to God's promises for their specific situation.

Spend some time as a group writing out prayers that include the biblical promises related to each member's personal situation. Have each member end their prayer with "Jesus, I trust in You."

Invite anyone who wishes to read their prayer to the group.

Questions for Reflection

1. What did it feel like to write your prayers to God?

2. What insights did you gain from chapter 6 that you could apply your own life?

3. Have you ever experienced a miracle in your own life? If so, describe it.

4. What is your biggest obstacle in receiving miracles or blessings from God? Is it unforgiveness, unbelief, worry, pride, fear, or doubt? Are you ready let these go?

5. In what area in your life do you need a miracle? Are you ready to begin renewing your mind and believing in God's promises in that situation?

Closing Prayer

Thank you, Lord for Your power, love, and word. Thank you, Lord, that we can cast all our cares upon You because You care so much for us. I thank you that You are a God of miracles, and we open up to receive those miracles in our own lives. Thank you, Lord, that Your hand and Your love and Your favor are upon us and our loved ones. As we are so richly blessed, may we continue to be a blessing to others and bring glory and honor to You. In Jesus' name.

RESOURCES

Books to Renew Your Mind and Uplift Your Soul

The Battle Plan for Prayer by Stephen and Alex Kendrick

Battlefield of the Mind by Joyce Meyers

Breaking Free by Beth Moore

Celebrate Recovery Bible and Workbook

Choose Joy by Kay Warren

The Circle Maker by Mark Batterson

Crash the Chatterbox by Steven Furtick

God Calling by A. J. Russell

God Is Able by Priscilla Shirer

Grace for the Good Girl by Emily P. Freeman

Grace Revolution by Joseph Prince

Practicing the Presence of God by Brother Lawrence

Imitation of Christ by Thomas à Kempis

Jesus Calling by Sarah Young

Jesus Is by Judah Smith

Life Recovery Bible and Workbook

Lifeline Kits by Kenneth and Gloria Copeland

Live, Love, Lead by Brian Houston

Man's Search for Meaning by Viktor E. Frankl

One Thousand Gifts by Ann Voskamp

Opening Our Hearts, Transforming our Losses by Al-anon Family Groups

The Purpose Driven Life by Rick Warren

Stronger by Clayton King

Sun Stand Still by Steven Furtick

Undaunted by Christine Caine

Unmerited Favor by Joseph Prince

You Are My Hiding Place by Amy Carmichael

Books for Parents of Struggling Teens

Boundaries with Teens by John Townsend

Come Back, Barbara by C. John Miller and Barbara Miller Juliani

The Power of Validation by Karyn D. Hall and Melissa Cook

Prayers and Promises for Worried Parents by Robert J. Morgan

Praying the Scriptures for Your Teenagers by Jodie Berndt

Prodigals and Those Who Love Them by Ruth Bell Graham

Teen Whisperer by Mike Linderman and Gary Brozek

Walking on Eggshells by Jane Isay

Audios

The Gospels, Charles Spurgeon

Lakewood Church Online

Parenting Teens, Christine Caine

Potential Church Online

Saddleback Church Online

Anything by TD Jakes, Joyce Meyers, Christine Caine, Jerry Savelle, Carolyn Savelle, Brian Houston, Charles Capp, Kenneth and Gloria Copeland, or Joel Osteen.

Videos

Living Well with a Diagnosis of Mental Illness, https://m.youtube.com/watch?v=IKhUH6KTQj0

Mental Health and the Church Summit, https://m.youtube.com/watch?v=atSyT0OPSwQ

Nick Vujicic, lifewithoutlimbs.org

Teen Extremes, https://m.youtube.com/watch?v=CJvPOgnaj1Q

Support

Please pray for guidance and consult with your physician or mental health professional before utilizing any of these resources. Utilizing any of these resources is your personal decision.

AA and NA
aa.org or na.org
Alcohol and drug addiction recovery

Al-anon
Alanon.org
Families and friends of alcoholics

Assistance and Counseling
Sheridan House Ministry
954-583-1552

Bible for Food Recovery
http://bibleforfood.org/
Telephone support for those struggling with food addictions and eating disorders

Borderline Personality Alliance
http://www.borderlinepersonalitydisorder.com/what-is-bpd/

Celebrate Recovery
http://www.celebraterecovery.com/
A Christ-based recovery program for the healing of hurts, hang-ups, and habits

Crisis Intervention
Text to 741741

Family Recovery Resources
786-859-4050
12stepfamily.com

First Call for Help: Broward County, Florida
24-Hour Suicide and Emotional Help Lines
Dial 211

First Call Line for Seniors
954-537-0211

Functional Neurology Rehab and Recovery

Carrick Institute
Training of professionals and treatment of neurological disorders
carrickinstitute.com

South Florida Integrative Health
Offers cutting edge treatment for ADHD, depression, anxiety, brain-based disorders, and immune system diseases
southfloridaintegrative.com

American Chiropractic Neurology Board
Doctor locator for chiropractic neurologists
acnb.org

GriefShare
griefshare.org
Group-based help dealing with the grief of loss

Grief Recovery
http://coffinca.wixsite.com/griefrecovery

House of Protection
Teen girl, Bible-based, recovery groups
954-562-6776
www.houseofprotection.org

Phone Friend
For kids to age thirteen
(954) 390-0486

NAMI
National Alliance of Mental Illness
NAMI.org
A wealth of resources for persons with mental illness and their families.

Recovery, Interventionist, and Educational Specialists for Troubled Teens and Adults

> Hayes Davidson and Associates
> hayes-davidson.com

> Martha Moses and Associates
> marthamoses.com

> BALM Family Recovery Resources
> familyrecoveryresources.com

Teen Hotline: Broward County, Florida
(954) 567-TEEN
(954) 567-8336
(954) 390-0485

Types of Therapy

DBT
Neurofeedback
EMDR Trauma Recovery

Prayer Lines

Daystar Prayer (800) 329-0029

Joel Osteen Prayer Line (888) 567-5635

KCM (817) 852-6000

Silent Unity (800) 669-7729, available twenty-four hours a day, and they continue to pray for thirty days

FINAL PRAYER

May the Lord cover you and your family in grace. May His favor surround you like a shield. And from the fullness of His grace, may you and your loved ones experience one blessing after another. In Jesus' name.

ACKNOWLEDGMENTS

My heart is so filled with gratitude for the many people who have blessed, inspired, and empowered me to write this book.

First and foremost, to my Lord and Savior, Jesus Christ: none of this would be possible without You.

To my extraordinary husband: thank you for your love, commitment and support. I love and respect you so.

To my children, Michael and Riley: I love you more than you'll ever know.

To Pastor Brian Vasil, Pastor Troy Grambling, and my Potential Church family: thank you for praying for me, equipping me, encouraging me, and believing in me.

To Dr. David Traster and Dr. Alexander Victoria: thank you for saving my life and changing my life.

To my dear friends, mastermind partners, and mighty prayer warriors, Cindy, Debbi, Janis, Renzo, Carolina, Dori, Mike, Sherry, Sylvia, Kina, Amy, Pam, and Lori: thank you for consistently reminding me of God's power, loving me so, and being spiritual giants.

To my wonderful editors, Janis, Ann, and Saundra: thank you for your extraordinary editorial skills.

To the team at EA Books Publishing: thank you for your publishing expertise that brought my book out into the world.

To my personal assistant, Adele: thank you for doing all you do so well.

To my parents: thank you for your unconditional love and acceptance.

To the Milam Family: thank you for loving me, entertaining me and praying me through so much.

And to my most precious fur baby, Gracie: thank you for the love, joy, and comfort you always provide.

NOTES

1. Viktor Frankl, *Man's Search for Meaning* (Boston: Beacon Press, 1959 [English version]).

2. Ken Blanchard and Phil Hodges *Lead Like Jesus: Lessons for Everyone from the Greatest Leadership Role Model of All Time* (Nashville: Thomas Nelson, 2005), 159.

3. Emily Perl Kingsley, "Welcome to Holland," Words of Inspiration and Hope, JourneyofHearts.org, http://www.journeyofhearts.org/kirstimd/holland.htm (last accessed April 19, 2017).

4. Herbert Lockyer, *All the Promises of the Bible* (Grand Rapids, MI: Zondervan, 1990).

5. Ann Voskamp, *One Thousand Gifts: A Dare to Live Fully Right Where You Are* (Grand Rapids, MI: Zondervan, 2011).

6. Ed Mazza, "Glenn Beck Sick with Mysterious Neurological Illness," *The Huffington Post*, November 11, 2014, http://www.huffingtonpost.com/2014/11/10/glenn-beck-sick_n_6136884.html (last accessed April 19, 2017).

7. Masaru Emoto, *The Hidden Messages in Water* (New York: Atria Books, 2005).

8. Ibid., "Water and Words," www.masaru-emoto.net/English/wter-crystal.html (last accessed January 18, 2017).

Grace Love Well Foundation

Grace Love Well Foundation is a 501(c)(3) nonprofit organization whose mission is to equip and encourage churches, pastors, Bible study leaders, and people across the country with inspiring resources to experience God's magnificent power, beauty, love, and presence.

One hundred percent of our proceeds support our charitable endeavors. These include donating and producing faith-building, God-glorifying books, Bible studies, and audio/video resources.

Visit us online at www.gracelovewell.org.

Lord, Show Me You Are Here

Lord, Show Me You Are Here is a visual retreat depicting how God epically shows up and off, a gift book filled with prayers, inspiration, and heaven-sent photography created as a refuge for experiencing the magnificent power, beauty, and love of God.

"This book is a must-read for those looking to grow in their walk with God. Through life-changing words and inspiring photography, each page draws the reader closer and closer to the majesty and beauty of our Lord. Looking for hope? Strength? A reminder of your value to God? It's all here . . . and so much more."

Pastor Brian Vasil, Pastoral Counselor, Potential Church

Order online at Amazon or www.gracelovewell.org

Made in the USA
Columbia, SC
05 September 2018